MW01152312

If You Lived Here
You'd be Home by Now

If You Lived Here
You'd be Home by Now

Life and Faith
and a Journey Home

Stan G. Duncan

If You Lived Here You'd Be Home by Now
Life and Faith and a Journey Home

Stan G. Duncan

© 2006 by Stan Duncan. All rights reserved.
Lulu Enterprises, Inc. | 3131 RDU Center, Suite 210 | Morrisville, NC 27560
919-459-5858|919-459-5867(fax)

For more information about Lulu Publishing Company, visit www.Lulu.com

PRINTED IN THE U.S.A.

FOR KEVIN, STAN, KARLA, AND BEV,
FOR THEIR ABILITY TO LIVE AND TEACH GRACE

Contents

Introduction

This is a collection of devotional essays for people who don't like syrup. I call them "honest faith" because they speak of finding God even when your loved one does in fact die; experiencing hope even when the cancer tests do come back positive; and trusting that God is just, even during a world and a war that has gone crazy. Perhaps they are best described as "in spite of" faith, as opposed to "triumphalist faith."

All of these stories have had their origins in other settings. Some were newsletter articles in various churches I have served. Some were sermons in those same churches. Several were articles written for the religion column I wrote for many years in a local newspaper, and some first appeared as commentaries on Public Radio.

In them, I'm trying hard not to shy away from the awfulness of death or the mysteriousness of suffering (or our frequent human culpability in both) because I don't think that would be honest to my faith or to God. And while most are not overtly political, some do come from the crucible of grinding social issues. That's where I live, and it would be equally dishonest to claim that there is some kind of theological wall between my world and my faith. Some stories, for example, take place in the poverty and conflict of Latin America where I have traveled frequently and have faithful friends of sterner stuff than I. One story follows my own family's difficult journey with my stepfather as he gradually slid from this life into the next. Another is about a carpenter in Oklahoma who lost his hand, his wife, and then his will to live, and nearly killed himself in grief, but who eventually discovered how to live again while working on a Habitat project arranged for him from a chance meeting with Jimmy Carter. And yet another tells of a successful clergy friend who "came out" to his church about his homosexuality and was then beaten nearly to death by his sexton.

Not every story is dark and wrenching. Many are lighter, some (I hope) are funny, and all are meant in the end to be uplifting. They are meant to encourage, empower, and strengthen. They are about real people whom I have known who have experienced real life, seldom washed and cleaned by Hollywood endings, but often chastened and renewed and empowered by their experiences.

Hopefully these stories will help the reader find and maintain faith even when conditions turn bad, experience inevitable hurt and then be healed. They don't pull back from pain but they also proclaim life in the midst of it.

We do indeed live in a wonderful world, as a song featured in one of these stories proclaims. But in my Christian tradition, one cannot get to the Resurrection without first going through the Crucifixion. Or as our Jewish friends might say, you can't get to the Promised Land without first spending time being lost in the wilderness. When Christians, or religious people of any stripe, surge too quickly to the joy of life in Christ, they often discover later that their faith is planted on shallow soil and will not serve them well when the inevitable storms of doubt and torment arrive.

In that sense, most of these essays can be considered survivor stories. They are embedded with joy and hope, they are filled with celebration and often humor. But it is a joy that is found and re-found on the other side of struggle.

Tornado Story

May 25, 1999

I talked to my mother the other day. It was right after the tornadoes tore through Oklahoma City destroying thousands of homes and killing dozens of people. I am originally from Oklahoma City and my mother still lives there. My old neighborhood was torn up pretty badly by the storm. From the news on TV I saw that our local hospital was damaged and my kids' high school was in ruins. My mom spent that night in a closet in the center of the house, wrapped in blankets, with candles, a radio, and a flashlight. She had a pan for the candles, she said, in case the tornado hit and the wax might drip on the carpet (Mom always was fond of neatness).

I had a hard time getting through in the beginning because all the lines were clogged with people like me trying to check in. When I finally got her, I wanted to know how she was doing, and was she hurt, and how was the neighborhood, but what she wanted to know was why God hated the people of Oklahoma City. "Mom," I said, not wanting to talk about that, and not wanting to sound like a pastor, "God doesn't hate you. These things just happen. It's nature, it's natural occurrences, and sometimes people get hurt."

But she wouldn't have it. "These things *don't* just happen," she said. "It happened here before at the Federal Building, and there's got to be a reason for it." She was thinking of the bombing of the Murrah Federal building in Oklahoma City in 1995. One hundred-fifty-six people died in that one, including some whom she knew personally. Natural evil is sometimes easier to explain away than human evil because a tornado is so much more impersonal than two cowboys who build a bomb out of fertilizer and murder children with it. "What is God trying to tell us with all this? It's just horrible."

"Mom," I said, "I don't think God is trying to tell you anything. I don't think God kills people to make a point."

"Well, where was he then? And those little kids up in Colorado, where was God when those kids were getting shot? Why'd he let those kids get killed?"

For a long time I couldn't answer. Pastors have a hard time under any circumstances in applying religious doctrine to something as awful as the suffering of children, but when the person we are talking to is also our mother, the task gets even harder. At what point will I say something a little too eloquent or poetic and she'll call me down for acting too uppity?

Letting her believe that God punishes sinners with tornadoes, or allowed the murder of teenagers in order to teach us a lesson seemed cruel. But if God didn't do it, then where was God when it happened? That was Mom's question. Does God just run off and let us kill each other, and not care about it? It's a question that every one of us should be asking I suppose, but one that few of us probably ever do. Where was God when the dying began?

So I blundered out something inconsequential to her, afraid of being too pious because she was after all my mother, and afraid of being too honest because of the horror of her questions. I don't think I satisfied her in the end.

When I hung up the phone, I recalled a decidedly *un*pious evening I spent years ago with an old Wycliffe Bible-translator high up in the mountainous *Ixil Nebaj* region of Guatemala many years ago. He and his wife and children had lived with this small village of Mayan Indians for over twenty years, translating the Bible into their Mayan dialect. While we talked, I noticed that mounted over his desk was a photo from a newspaper of about a dozen little children standing with their arms straight out at their sides. We had been eating dinner and laughing before I noticed it, but when I asked him about it he grew very quiet. "Those were *Quichéan* children," he said, very slowly. "They were doing the cross of Jesus."

"What does that mean?" I asked.

"They believe that if you hold your hands out when you are hurting, you can touch the wounds of Jesus. Then Jesus suffers with you and alongside you, and your own pain is then not so bad." He stopped for a moment and rubbed his face, thinking. "It's a common tradition among the Christian Mayans here. When God suffers alongside you, in the midst of your own hurt, then in some mysterious way your hurt becomes God's hurt. Your pain doesn't go away, but it gets taken up into God and you are strengthened. They do this when something awful is about to happen because it gives them strength."

"But what awful thing could be happening to those little kids," I asked. They looked pretty comfortable to me.

"See those shadows off on the side?" he asked. I did, but not very well. "Those shadows are from the ends of the rifles of about fifty Guatemalan soldiers. They were "cleansing" this village. They were in the process of killing every person in town, and would have finished it, except this photographer got the picture."

"All of them?" I asked. "The children too?"

"As I recall the story," he said, "every child was murdered just after this photo was taken. They were buried in that pit in back of them." He took the photo down so that we could look at it more closely. "But look at their faces," he said. "They're smiling. They won, the army lost. God's suffering was right there in the middle of them, every second."

I called my mother up a couple of days later and told her that story. She was silent for a moment after I finished and then she started crying. She said, "That night of the tornado? I thought I was going to die. I wanted to pray to God to save me, but I knew that God wouldn't stop the storm just to rescue me. So I prayed that he would just be there with me if it happened. Maybe not change anything, but just be with me. And you know what?"

"What?" I said.

"He did. And I wasn't afraid."

If You Lived Here

Karla Had a Baby

August, 2005

She called us first on Sunday evening, but we missed the call and had to call her back. No one was home so we left a message. The next day she called again while we were gone and days of agonizing phone tag passed until finally she broke through and made the announcement. "He came!" she yelled. "He was early, but he's beautiful." Karla had a baby.

We danced, we cried, we celebrated. It was a glorious day. How big is he, how much does he weigh? When did he come? We wanted to ask every question we could think of. We wanted to hold him and love him, and welcome him into the world.

As some kind of statement of faith and hope and love for a future that can no longer be predicted, Karla had a baby.

Iraq is in flames, with hundreds of our young people and thousands of theirs dying day after day after day. Fear of violent acts of terror stalk us with continuing ferocity and drive us deeper and deeper into a reactionary shell of defensiveness and rigidity. Darfur and Niger melt in malevolent civil wars and famines that threaten to drag down the whole of northern Africa. And Karla had a baby.

In a world so full of heartache and hate and death and oppression, what meaning can there be in a young couple who so defy the evening news that they believe in putting out new life in the midst of the carnage? The future is so unsure. The potential for disaster is so high. But magically and mysteriously, people still have an innate spiritual gift to look at each other and believe that one more new child in the world can be good.

In my ministry I have known countless people who were ill or old or hurt or lonely; scarred or crippled or diseased or frightened. There is a tremendous potential for despair. Life is fragile and frail, and at any minute it can be taken away from any of us. And yet, Karla had a baby.

There's no accounting for faith. There's no longer as much of a need to have children to take care of us in our old age as there was two hundred years ago. No longer a need for them to work our farms for us. No moral need. No practical need. But still, with a mysterious, nonsensical, built-in belief that love is worth gambling on and tomorrow can be better than today, people have babies. How can you explain that?

Perhaps God, in a burst of compassion, built into the DNA of human creation the belief that love can trump fear. Perhaps God created us to defy logic and live as though hope can be rational?

There's no accounting for this. No justification. No reason to believe that there is a reason for this. Life creaks along, moaning toward its ultimate demise. Under the best of situations it is full of slips and falls and broken bones, ruptured spleens, cancered lungs, and a final disease that saps our strength, our will, and finally our lives. Under the worst of situations it is full of disease, hunger, oppression, war, and death. There are joys along the way, but in the end nobody gets out alive. We all lose in the end. So why try? Why fight? Why have a baby?

But Karla had a baby.

It Was the Building That Saved Him

S ome years ago, when I lived in Oklahoma, I helped found a local chapter of Habitat for Humanity. There were just three of us in the beginning: A friend of mine did the organizing, I did media, and this nice woman named Marge something-or-other was the treasurer. One day, soon after we got it started, we had a big gathering that was part fundraiser and part get-acquainted meeting. My church hosted it and put on the refreshments. They had me staff the punch bowl to greet and smile pleasantly at the newcomers because I couldn't do much else. While I was standing there doing my job, I met a pleasant looking gentleman who introduced himself as "George," and seemed right at home, though I hadn't yet met him. I noticed he was missing his right hand, though he didn't seem to have any trouble filling his cup at the bowl.

He told me that he had been a carpenter all his life. Lived outside the city in a small town whose name I've now forgotten. He said he used to drink something terrible, and that one day he'd gotten drunk and crashed his truck into the storefront window of a bank, and was in the hospital for over a week. Among other things, he had rammed his hand through the windshield of the truck and cut it off. They rushed him to the emergency room, but it was too damaged and they couldn't save it. On top of that, he didn't have very good insurance, and the hospital billed him and the bank sued him. He was ruined.

After that, he pretty much shut down. He and his wife managed to save their little home, and he had Social Security and she had some pension, but his life, so far as he was concerned was over. He said he got started sitting in a lounge chair watching TV with a "clicker" for hours and hours every day. He fell into what we would think of as a deep depression, though he never called it that. He just felt dead and was waiting around for the end of life to catch up with how his heart already felt.

Periodically his wife would come in and plead with him to get up and do something to get his life going again. He wouldn't move. He could no longer work, so for him he lost not only his job, but also his manhood. He was no longer a good provider, so what good was he? Nothing, he thought, so he just drank beer and clicked channels and avoided letting his mind function.

He said that now and then he'd say a few words to his wife during dinner, or at night, but more or less he let his life slide into a deep pit that he couldn't get out of. One day, some years after the accident happened he remembered vaguely that his wife packed up some things and said good-bye. He absently wondered what she was up to but didn't think about it. Then that evening he listened and looked around and realized that she was gone. She was really gone. Her things were gone. A note was left. She wouldn't be back. She wrote she had tried to help him, to talk to him, to love him, but he wouldn't let her. She had failed. She mourned, she cried, she prayed, but she couldn't stay.

For a while he responded simply by falling deeper into his despair. Aside from eating and sleeping, which he did poorly and sporadically, he barely moved. Just sat in his chair drinking and clicking. Then one day he saw Jimmy Carter on TV. It's been some time now, but he recalled that Jimmy was in Philadelphia rehabbing old houses. It was a special day, a disabled-working-on-the-houses day. All the people in the work crew had lost hands or feet, or were otherwise crippled up, bent over, or in wheel chairs. He saw this crowd and distantly saw himself. Here were people worse off than he was, and they were building houses for Jesus.

He pulled himself up from his chair, took a shower, packed some food, crawled into his old camper, and took off for Plains Georgia, to Jimmy Carter's house. Without a thought as to whether he could actually walk into the home of a former president, he just drove.

Twoday's drive later he drove up to the Carter house, and sure enough there were official looking people in front, but far from keeping him out, they invited him in. He went up to the door, knocked, and a moment later Rosalyn Carter came to the door. He stumbled and stammered and told her his story and she said, Just a minute. And then President Carter appeared, in a bathrobe, holding a cup of coffee. He invited George in. The three of them sat at the Carter breakfast table and talked for over an hour. George told his story, and they listened. They prayed together, shared Scripture together, and then in the end Jimmy got on the phone and called some people he knew who planned projects for Habitat to see what they could do to set George up with a work project sometime soon.

George did it. In fact, he spent all of that summer, and the better part of the rest of his life, traveling around from house to house, helping work parties on Habitat houses.

And there he was across from me by the punch bowl telling me his story. I was moved, I was humbled. It was a great story. "It was the work what saved me," I remember him saying. "When I was rebuilding them houses, I was actually rebuilding my life. If I hadn't started working for Jesus, I would've died."

I said "That's a wonderful story. But…" I was cautious about asking this. "What about your wife? What happened there?" I was afraid that that wouldn't be a happy ending.

He beamed. "In fact you met her." I took a breath. "You met her right over there. That was her there who gave you your name tag as you came through the door. He called out, and sure enough Marge, the treasurer, looked up and smiled a lovely smile at us and waved. George beamed again. Sure enough, putting houses together he put his life together. It was working for Jesus what saved him.

If You Lived Here

Salvadoran Advent

December, 1987

Years ago, during the 1980s I spent several months in El Salvador doing research for a masters thesis in economic development. During that time I traveled through several villages in the northern part of the country that had been ravaged from the brutal and evil fighting of the civil war. In those days the United States was involved in a number of wars in Central America, and, as it happens, I was involved in a few personal wars inside my own soul over whether I should stay in the church or become an economist working for economic just in countries like El Salvador.

I was traveling with a tall, red-haired, lapsed Catholic, named Warick Frye, who was a journalist from Australia. We were there doing research on "repopulation villages." Those were towns being resettled by people who had been driven out of the country by the military during the early years of repression. Frye was doing a photo essay, and I was writing a book on the politics of the region, but I think that actually I was there searching for something deeper, something perhaps more spiritual, though I didn't know it at the time.

The people of the repopulated village we were visiting had been hiding in refugee camps in Honduras for over a decade, but they finally decided that they could only bring true peace to their country by returning to their roots, by coming home. They renamed their village, appropriately, *Las Vueltas*, "The (place of)Return."

We stumbled into Las Vueltas somewhat by accident. We had been studying another town some miles away and had heard that the army had mined all of the roads around the town, and that if we left, we'd have to hike over a mountain to get out. It was a terrifying thought. A guide volunteered to take the two of us and a supply of food through the woods and up over the mountain. It was cold and wet and windy, and we were not dressed nor in shape for the walk. For two excruciating days we walked, until we finally dropped down into what we thought would be the safety of Las Vueltas.

When we arrived, we were exhausted and surprised to find them welcoming us like visiting dignitaries. The mayor and half his council came out to greet us. What they told us was that this "free" village and the land around it had just been sold out from under the populace by the government to an international agribusiness corporation for the planting and export of corn. The government never approved of the people moving back home, so it gave them a deadline and ordered them to abandon the town or face dire consequences. The village had known of the sale for some time but didn't believe their government could do such a thing, so they voted to stay and hold their ground. Frye and I arrived, weary and wet, the very day the final deadline passed.

The people who had greeted us with such enthusiasm were hoping that if they sent word back to the capital that there were *internacionistas*, "internationals" staying with them, the government might back off on its threats to depopulate the town. That's why they were so happy to see us, but we found out later that their happiness was ill-founded.

For lodging (and perhaps safety) we were escorted to the local Catholic church where we were warmly received by a wonderful nun named Sister Loretta. She said she didn't want to alarm us, but the strongest, sturdiest building in the compound was the sanctuary, and she had set us up with some cots to stay there. We were alarmed.

She brought us some food, and blankets, and warm hugs. And she wished us God's peace. "Tomorrow is the first day of Advent," she said.

"The Christ Child will be journeying to us. This time above all other times, pray for peace." Frye, the atheist, and I the questioner, both asked why? Would it change what might happen tonight? She smiled. "No," she said. "But it might change your hearts."

She left, and had barely returned to her own quarters when a huge explosion went off in the street, and for a moment the sanctuary was bathed in light. It was followed by a second and a third, all powerful explosions and flashes of light. We rushed out the front doors and saw a bank not thirty feet away from us in ruins. The sky was dotted with the lights of helicopters swooping down onto the town. The duly elected democratic government of El Salvador was attacking its own citizens to drive them out of their homes.

Frye and I ran back into the church. Our cots were useless. The small church had little furniture and few places for refuge. "Let's try under the altar," he said. "You're the religious one; maybe you can make it do some good." My religious credentials didn't seem particularly strong at that point but I joined him under it anyway. It was solid thick marble—the only thing in the sanctuary of much value or strength. Hanging above it was a giant crucifix, a plaster Jesus on a cross that stood at least ten feet tall. We crouched together under the altar.

For hours we heard the same frightening pounding in the streets, punctuated by sounds of people running and occasionally crying, and dozens of dogs barking. I hid there, in overwhelming horror, in a tight ball, occasionally adding my own cries to those of the streets. Later we learned that nearly the entire village fled for the night and hid in creek beds and behind boulders, and that miraculously no one died. But at the time all I could be aware of was the sounds of screaming and running, and the explosions that were endless and relentless. Every moment grew more frightening than the last. The longer the destruction went on, the less likely it seemed that we could possibly live through it.

Once there was a pause for several minutes and we cautiously started to crawl out of our sacred refuge. But just then there was another blinding explosion and the front doors of the church blew off their hinges and straight into the sanctuary. Window glass shattered and flew across the room. We dove back under the altar just as the giant crucifix came loose from one of its wires and swung down crashing into the marble side of the altar. Another explosion, and the crucified body of Christ broke free of its wires, and fell down beside us, creating almost another wall of protection from the ravages of the outside, and he stayed there for the rest of the night.

On into the night, in terror and exhaustion, we heard bombs pounding and pounding, shaking the walls of the church when they grew near. Again and again, on and on, endlessly they exploded, as we hid trembling under a marble altar at the plaster feet of Jesus. Not knowing what to do, I shook, and crouched, and cried, and finally prayed. I prayed for a peace that I could never have prayed for in a calm suburb of North America. I prayed for a peace that I would never have been able to understand until that night, a peace that might not change the world, but that might change me in the midst of it.

And eventually I found myself resting, almost calmly, even in the midst of the endless evil falling around us. In my weariness, I squirmed over to the crucifix and leaned against it. I rested my head in the curve of Jesus' foot. I put my chin on a plaster spike ringed by a trickle of plaster blood where it entered Jesus' foot. And I slept.

I don't know how long I slept, but it was a long, deep, and restful sleep. A sleep driven by a mixture of exhaustion and fear and peace. I somehow felt, in a way that I still can't explain, that whatever happened, it would all be okay. Finally, sometime into the morning I was aroused. I looked up and saw sunlight shining in through the windows of the sanctuary. Sister Loretta and several others were busy cleaning up the debris. The villagers all across the town were returning to their homes and opening their shops, doing their best to show their government that they were still not afraid. They were showing that by returning to their homes they had found their peace. Perhaps so had I. My friend Warick Frye was standing over me holding a broom and smiling grandly. "Hey, guy, wake up," he said. "It's morning. You're alive. There's work to do. It's Advent."

Real Good Looker

Summer had finally arrived around our house, and the weather was pleasant enough, for the first time, to get out and do a little work on the lawn. Lawn care is a difficult task, but in our household, I am always aided by the sage advice and council of our cat Geraldine.

The first thing that Geraldine has always taught me is how to pace myself. She advises that whenever I have one of those days when I feel full of energy and can't wait to get outside and tackle all those jobs around the house, I should just lie down for a few minutes for a nap and eventually the feeling will go away.

She's also very good about helping me keep some of my important decisions in perspective. For example, I often worry too much about the relative merits of edging my lawn with a weed eater or a full-blown edging machine. Or I may fret over whether I should continue the thick patch of Zoysia grass that has taken over the center of my lawn or encourage the fescue and rye grass that surrounds it and grows well in the shade but isn't as thick and lush as the Zoysia. These are the questions that I ponder for some time because each decision has long-term implications.

Geraldine has taught me to not take those questions so seriously. She has questions too, but hers tend to be like whether it is better to sleep in a sunbeam on the grass or in the shade on the porch. Those are important questions also, but Geraldine knows that if she discovers she has made a mistake, it won't be the end of the world, and she knows how to live with the results of her decisions.

The most important thing that Geraldine has taught me is how to look. I thought I "looked" good before I met Geraldine, but she has taught me much. She is a real good "looker" and I'm envious of that. I have seen her sit out on the deck for two and three hours at a time just looking. She is great at it. I get edgy and fidgety and overly concerned about the affairs of my life or the world, and then I see Geraldine out there on the deck looking. I'm sure she is concerned about whether the bills will be paid on time or whether the copy machine will last until a capital campaign or whether Congress will pass a universal health-care plan, but she has learned how to handle these things with grace and ease, simply by looking. One sees much when one learns to look. She has seen rain falling, snow melting, sun shining, birds singing, squirrels playing, and flowers blooming. There is much that is "out there" that teaches us how to live "in here." Geraldine taught me that.

Nowadays, when the computer breaks down, or the city's town meeting is canceled, or a funeral service has drained me of all of my energy and juices, I go to the window, loosen my tie, take off my shoes, lean back in my chair, and I look. I think of Geraldine when I look, and appreciate her wisdom. At least I think I am looking. At least that's what I tell people when the phone rings a half hour or so later and the person on the phone asks me why my voice sounds so groggy and sleepy. I tell them I've been looking.

La Ceiba

December 12, 1998

Following the destruction of Hurricane Mitch

I N just one week, back in 1998, a little town that I used to call home—and a great many of its residents, whom I dearly loved—died.

Back in the late eighties, I lived in a sweet little seaport town called "La Ceiba," on the northern Caribbean coast of Honduras. It was named after a rare tropical tree called the "Ceiba," which seems to grow forever with huge intertwining branches that—according to the legend—held down the earth to keep it secure in the universe. The roots of the tree seemed to reach to the center of the earth, where the center of God's spirit resided. We had one such tree in our town, and it was breathtaking. It was down by the beach in a park that I passed by whenever I would walk from my apartment to a friend's house near the water. On the way to her house, I would occasionally stop and admire the massive Ceiba tree, in all its glory, holding down the earth and protecting it from the various evils that want to blow it away. It was so large that it was hard to imagine anything dislodging its hold on the ground that it was there to secure. Its branches soared upward and outward into a magnificent canopy, broad and flat, and harpies—the largest of all eagles—would perch on them and study our behaviors from above, searching for prey.

My job in those days was to do research on the work of development agencies in Honduras for a master's thesis I was writing in economics. But in the process I met and loved—and now miss—an enormous number of people and places. I lived in a tiny upstairs apartment on Colon Avenue in a gorgeous old Spanish villa with terraces and patios and hanging plants. My bedroom was on the second floor with a magnificent floor-to-ceiling, bricked-in arched window overlooking a busy Caribbean street scene below. I had a lush forest of nationalities and races that poured through the street below me all through the day and most of the night, buying and selling, begging and badgering one another until their faces and voices began to blend like a choir in some kind of modern abstract harmony. Often when I got to bed at night I would turn off the light and open the curtains and lie there looking out at the lights and listening to the horns of the buses and the taxis singing to one another until I finally fell asleep.

My landlord was Mauricio Benza, a dignified, aging, thin lipped Spaniard, with a pencil thin black mustache and an always present bow tie. I loved the looks of him because he reminded me of all of the Hollywood movie depictions of old world Spanish aristocracy. He had a slight smell about him of someone who wore just a touch too much cologne or hair cream. His hair had a metallic smoothness to it and I suspected that he used the better part of a bottle of Wildroot Cream Oil to get it to lie down like that.

Next door to the villa was my barber, Alfonso. I was warned before I ever went to see him that he was not fond of the influence that the American military was having on Honduras in those days, so I confess I lied to him and told him I was from Great Britain and we became fast friends. I loved Alfonso. He was an immigrant from Italy, and his Spanish was as bad as mine. We could talk well together because neither of us knew how to use big words and complicated sentences.

I remember too that Alfonso's shop also had that same smell to it that Mauricio my landlord had, and I often wondered if Alfonso was the supplier for Mauricio's pungent hair products.

Down the street from Alfonso was the *Parque Infantil*, the "Children's Park." When I would get home early, I liked to go there and sit on a bench and watch the kids play while I fed the pigeons. Across the street was a great place to eat called *La Pizza Barrata*, "The Cheap Pizza." The owners not only let you choose your own ingredients, but also had tables around the walls of the dining room where customers could roll out the dough and bake their pizzas themselves. It was a great hit with the kids.

One day while I was sitting on my bench feeding some leftover pizza to pigeons, a man named Guillermo came up to me and begged for some money. I was nervous about beggars, so I lied to him and said I didn't have any. Undaunted, he said, Well, then, would you like to buy a map? I thought about it and said that yes, I would like to buy a map. So, I took some of the money I had just told him I didn't have and I bought my first map of Honduras. I still have it.

Over the next few weeks Guillermo found me many times, and each time we repeated the same litany. I didn't always buy his products (I didn't always feel good about where he might have obtained them) but I enjoyed his company and his humor and his spunk. Off and on he tried to sell me tourist postcards, seashells, movie tickets, and even discount coupons from The Cheap Pizza. We shared the pizzas and had a great time. One day he met me in the park and announced that he had found a cat and wanted to keep it, so I gave him about ten dollars in Honduran *Limpira* to buy cat food and milk. He told me it was a loan, but I didn't believe it. I didn't even think about it anymore until many months later when I had moved back to Tegucigalpa and I got a letter that Mauricio forwarded to me. It was from Guillermo, thanking me for the loan, apologizing for the delay, and repaying the loan. In the envelope was a bundle of Cheap Pizza coupons in a rubber band, the value of which was about ten dollars.

Outside of La Ceiba there were a number of clinics set up over many years by Dr. William Climer, a United Church of Christ medical missionary in Honduras. Bill could have made a fine living anywhere in the world, but for thirty years he lived, worked, and raised his family among the poorest of the poor in Honduras. In town I knew a hardware store owner named Raul Madrigo, over on a street called the *Avenida de La Republica*, who grew up receiving free medical care from one of Bill's clinics. Now he gives one day a week volunteering at another clinic in the poor *Garifuna* Indian community.

If You Lived Here

About a block down Colon Avenue on the corner of Thirteenth Street there was a real live Dunkin' Donuts, where I ate breakfast almost every morning. It was a little touch of North America in an otherwise very Caribbean looking world. It looked and felt almost like any Dunkin' Donuts in the states, except that the coffee had a blackened ruddy texture to it and tasted something like a mixture of tar and charcoal. Honduran coffee is a serious drink for serious drinkers, and they are amazed at the weakened, pale fluid that passes for coffee in the States. It took me weeks before I could get my tolerance for caffeine up to Honduran levels, and I finally prided myself on my ability to down two whole cups at one sitting, though I'm sure it did terrible damage to my blood pressure each time I did it.

I got into trouble at that Dunkin' Donuts one time, on my last day in La Ceiba. I had finished my work and was moving to Tegucigalpa, the capital of Honduras. I got to the bus station early, bought my ticket, put all of my luggage on the bus, and then went down the street to Dunkin' Donuts to have one last muffin and cup of caffeinated tar. But when I got back, less than an hour later, the bus had already filled up and was taking off. I waved at the driver to stop, but he refused. He'd gotten his load and was leaving early, even if my things were on his bus! But I couldn't send all of my worldly possessions off on a strange bus without me, so I jumped onto the ladder on the back of the bus, crawled along the top holding onto the luggage racks, and then slid down the side by the front door. I put one foot on the running board and one on the right fender, and held onto the rear view mirror, and rode that way, like Indiana Jones, for about two hours until we finally came to a another coastal town called Tela where the driver let some passengers off and nonchalantly let me on.

Inside I collapsed in a rumpled, dirty, smelly, heap of exhaustion and dust across the aisle from a very proper-looking little girl in a prim pink dress who was reading a book. She looked up at me and over to her mother next to her, and then back to me. She said, "We're going to visit my grandmother in Tegucigalpa, and we're all dressed up." She twisted up her nose like she was sniffing the air. "And I guess you're not going to go visit anybody."

* * * * * *

On Monday, October 26, 1998, Hurricane Mitch began to threaten the northern shores of Honduras and Nicaragua. It was huge at first, but for a while it dissipated and people in La Ceiba and other coastal towns breathed more easily. Then, just as they were beginning to relax, it made a dramatic turn downward right into the coast, and there it stalled for six days, dropping as much as four inches of rain per hour. Fifty rivers overflowed their banks in the area. In La Ceiba, every house and building from the Caribbean shoreline up the hill for twenty blocks through the *Parque Infantil* was covered in water in the first two days. My friend's simple home on the beach was gone. The villa I lived in was gone. The Dunkin' Donuts was gone. The barber shop, Cheap Pizza, and movie house were all gone. The mighty Ceiba tree, holding onto the earth to keep it secure, was completely buried in water and sand. Many of the rural clinics that Dr. Climer had labored to build for so many years, were gone. Destroyed. Washed away. In the first four days seventy-thousand people were evacuated from their homes. Ironically, when the storm was building, people bought out the local stores of their medical and food supplies, and then later, when their homes washed away, there was no food left for the people who were brought in to the shelters.

Days later when helicopters finally began arriving to take in some of the survivors, they saw rooftops with people lying dead on top of them. They found babies whose mothers had tried to save them by tying them to the tops of trees to protect them, but they were dead. They had survived the storm but then died of hunger.

One man survived by breaking open a hot-water tank and drinking from it. A four-year-old-neighbor girl washed in and lodged into the window of his house. He could wrap her up, but he couldn't get her out. So he saved her life by getting drinks of fresh water from the tank in his mouth and squirting it from his mouth into hers. Another man was caught in a mud slide next to his house. He heard the roar of the rain and the mud coming down onto him, so he lashed himself to a tree to protect himself, but the tree and his entire house were carried away with the water. He floated for over ten miles tied to the tree before he was lodged into a mud bank and the rope broke free. His feet were buried deep into the mud, but it broke both his legs, and he lay there for two more days waiting for someone to come and dig him out.

The death toll across Honduras rose into the thousands. It is estimated that one out of every three buildings in the *entire* country was destroyed! Every major road was destroyed, every airport. Every major power line. Seventy percent of the economic production of the nation was ruined. At least twelve-thousand people, real people, died. Thirteen thousand were unaccounted for. Over one-million people were put into temporary shelters. At least a million-and-a-half more were made homeless.

* * * * * *

I have two purposes in telling you this story. The first is to help you get a feeling for the real people with names who died or have been lost in this tragedy. When people die far-away it's terrible, but we don't feel for them because we don't know them. I don't know anybody in Rwanda, or Darfur, or Palestine, or Afghanistan. It is hard to know the true impact of suffering and dying until you know somebody there. I wanted you to know that these people are not statistics but real people, good people, kind people, and they all died. And I miss them.

The second thing I wanted to say is that God did not create Hurricane Mitch. There is a perverted, cruel theology that says that if someone dies it is because God did it, either to punish us, or to teach us a lesson. I hear it often: "God had a reason for 'taking' my mother." "Why did God 'take' my father?" But that belief is wrong. God doesn't kill people. Storms, hurricanes, accidents, and human sin kill people. God is not in the destruction, but in the healing. God is not in the breaking, but in the mending.

God did not cause a teenage drunken driver to kill my father and his fiancée years ago on a highway the week before their wedding. God did not cause my stepfather to suffer and die of a series of ghastly strokes that weakened him until he could only die to find relief.

God is indeed in the midst of suffering, but as its resolution, not its cause. God is in its healing. God is in the relief workers, the doctors, the volunteers, and in the heroic acts of people who saved their neighbors and rescued survivors. God's act of creation is for good, not evil, and when the creation falls, God is in the pain working for the best possible outcome of.

I worried and cried for my friends. I tried to contact them and was unable to reach most of them. I also prayed to God for them, not with anger but that they could reach out to God's spirit and experience strength and courage in it, whether in this world or the next.

Perhaps in one sense God is like the mighty Ceiba tree. News reports say that when the waters receded, they finally found it—beaten and damaged—but still standing. They say that throughout the storm and its horrendous destruction, the tree gave strength to the community and all of the people who lived around it, in part because it too had suffered, right in the midst of their suffering, right alongside their pain, and in the end, battered and bruised, it never released its hold on the earth.

If You Lived Here

If You Lived Here, You'd be Home by Now

I had intended to tell a story that was autobiographical, but instead I think I'll tell one that's about me.

The autobiographical story that I won't tell had to do with a time when I used to work at the University of Massachusetts at Boston and commuted with about 1.5 million others back and forth from the suburban town of Arlington every day. On the way home, just after we would leave the downtown area and pull out onto Storrow Drive along the Charles River, traffic would invariably grind to a halt and we would all have to rest for a while in front of a set of "toney" condominiums that had a big sign out front extolling its virtues to the commuters. In addition to reasonable prices and views of the Charles, it also said, a bit smugly, "If You Lived Here, You'd be Home by Now."

I hated that sign. I hated it most because it was true. On my way home, I would pass dozens of stoplights, hundreds of buses, and thousands of cars, but if I had only lived closer to the "center" I would have found my home already.

Being "home" was true geographically and it was also true personally. I spent years and years of my life searching for some kind of enriching, exciting experience that would bring me happiness or fulfillment or peace, or who knows what, but the truth always was that if I could just learn to live closer to the "center," where Christ has always resided, waiting for me, then I'd have been "home by now."

A couple of years ago someone told me that vandals had slipped onto the condo's grounds late at night and thrown black and white paint all over the sign. It was defaced so badly that the owners were considering taking it down. The police surmised that teenagers had done it, but I never believed that. I always figured that it was a bunch of middle-aged white guys in suits who snuck in there in the dead of night and threw copy machine toner and "white-out" all over it. They finally got so fed up looking at the sign that they went over the edge and took it out in a midnight commando raid.

Do you remember the ancient medieval legend of the Holy Grail, the one about the guy who spent his entire life searching for the magical Grail used at the Last supper? I don't want to write in footnotes, but Joseph Campbell, the great scholar of myths, says that the story of the quest for the Grail is the quintessential myth of western civilization. On the other hand, Robert Johnson, a Jungian psychoanalyst, has said that more than that, it is the quintessential myth of western *males*. I'm no expert, but I'm inclined to go with Johnson on that one.

According to the story, the Grail is the very cup that Christ drank from, and it supposedly contained drops of blood taken from his side when he died. If someone found it, he (and it has to be a "he" if this is to be a male myth) would receive total self-discovery and spiritual self-awareness. The legend is that a young boy named Parsifal, who lived on the grounds of the castle where it was kept, stumbled across the Grail one night and almost touched it. He came within inches of it. But the closer he got to touching the mysterious source of self-discovery, the more frightened he became (if that isn't a guy thing, I don't know what is). So he turned and ran away, out of the castle, out into the woods, and didn't look back until he was totally lost.

He was remorseful that he had turned away in fear from his near-discovery experience, and so he spent the rest of his life trying to find his way back home again to the hidden castle one more time to touch the Grail and finally get it right. He traveled for years in search of the Grail. He became a knight and was famous throughout the land, wearing dashing (and symbolically very thick) armor, and vanquishing every foe of truth and beauty. He carried a mighty shield and spear, and beat every enemy in battle. He was even honored by King Arthur himself for his bravery. But in the end, he still could not find his way back home and to the Grail.

Finally, when he grew very old, tired, defeated, and lost, he stumbled into a monastery on Good Friday. He was weak and discouraged and decided that his life would never be complete because he had never found the Holy Grail, the source of all meaning. He asked them if he could just take Communion with the simple monks and live with them in peace. When he told the monks his story, a wise man of the monastery stepped forward and said simply, "The grail? Oh, it's just down the road about two kilometers, turn left, and across the bridge. It's not far."

Parsifal was shocked. "Do you mean," he said, "that I could have gone just a little bit further and finally found it?"

"I don't know," said the monk. "You have to know where to look. We've seen you pass by our gates about thirty times over the past few years. We wondered what you were up to. It seems you've been riding around in circles pretty much all your life."

He collapsed in joy and heartache. He'd been circling the castle that kept the Grail all this time, but didn't know it. He'd never been more than fifteen miles from the Grail ever since he began his search. It seems he had done everything to find self-realization except look close to home.

I'm not sure, but I think the point of the story is that if he had only known where he really lived, he'd have been home by now.

If You Lived Here

Cat Theologies

Our second cat is named Mikey. I realize that that is a pretty abysmal name for a female cat, but, then, one could argue that cats are a fairly abysmal creature to begin with, so I suppose it fits. The name came about because no one could think of a good name for her when she was a kitten. Eventually, someone (history does not record who it was) said, "Well, if nobody comes up with anything soon, I'll name her 'Mikey,' after the kid in the cereal commercials who would eat *anything*. The description seemed appropriate, because the cat would in fact eat anything, so the name stuck.

I've always suspected that Mikey's name affected her personality, because she became the neighborhood tough guy. Before I married into her family, she had already had her front claws removed to protect the world from her rowdy ways. Cats are not usually on my most-favored-animal list—I had dogs when I was a kid—but my wife made it clear when if we got married the wife came with cats or else the husband would never be married to the wife...or something like that.

It's been interesting watching the two cats interact over the years. Both of them are actually quite religious in their own way, but they express their faith very differently, based on their different traditions. Geraldine, I was told, came from a very proper Lutheran family and she has some deeply ingrained habits and beliefs that have never changed in her years with us. Attentiveness to ritual and the sacraments is the clear way for her to find God. She tried for months to get Pastor Steinhart from St. Marks Lutheran down the street to come by and offer her Holy Eucharist, but so far the pastor hasn't seen the wisdom (or the humor) in dropping by. Geraldine did get drunk one night, and we turned on Father Butler on the cable access station and told her he was Lutheran. She didn't know the difference and had a wonderful experience.

Mikey, on the other hand, was a Unitarian Universalist, and she tends to have a much more activist religion. For her, God is found in the prowl of life. She roams restlessly throughout the house and yard searching for truth, always certain that inside the next cardboard box or overturned watering can there might be a clue to the meaning of existence. For Mikey, faith is expressed in intellectual curiosity. For Geraldine it is in rigid adherence to orthodox, seasoned patterns of worship: Food, sleep, yawn, beg. Food, sleep, yawn, beg. These are the means of grace through which God is known.

Mikey is much more of an adventurous mystic than Geraldine. She likes to meditate on the interdependent web of all creation (found usually hanging from the back of the stairs in the basement). For Geraldine, God is more tangible and found in the immediate acts of faith: reciting the creeds and confessions, celebration of the sacraments, and attempting to eat one's body weight in cat food at least once each day. To illustrate the difference, Mikey is convinced that rolling on her back on the driveway in the summer sun is the best way to become one with everything. During this ecstatic state, bowls of fish, milk, and live mice could be set around her and she would not be able to recognize them because her heart would be so filled with the Ground of Being and the unity of all of creation in the soul of the spirit of life. Geraldine would eat the fish.

On the other hand, Geraldine's conservative, high-church religion has served her well in life. There is much wisdom in her theology of decency and order. Boundaries were created by God for the purpose of preserving the sacred gift of life itself. Crossing those boundaries is not only sin, it also risks destroying a part of God's good creation. For example, never fight with a raccoon. In altercations between a cat and even the smallest, most benign raccoon, it is never the cat who wins, and then one of God's most important creations is lost.

Geraldine's faith has real dignity. It is calm, peaceful, and deeply rooted in history and tradition, which contrasts greatly with Mikey's more intellectual, universalist, almost chaotic faith. Who am I to say that one way of finding God is better than the other? When Geraldine prays it is for calm and rest from the busy-ness of life. When Mikey prays it is for new insights and new accomplishments. It may be that Mikey's outward-directed faith is a result of guilt over a past that she is unable to forget. She had an unfortunate problem with catnip in her youth which still burdens her and drives her. Geraldine believes one should never brood over the past. It lacks decorum, denies God's real forgiveness of sins, and it makes you look too much like humans.

As different as the two cats are, one might expect that they would never get along. But actually they are models for how persons with vastly different opinions and lifestyles could live together and love each other. Mikey the activist and Geraldine the pietist make a nice couple. They remind me of two old women who have been together for so many years that they now know each other's every mood and feeling and don't have to ask about it any longer. They probably would have gotten married years ago but Geraldine's church would never hear of such a thing. So instead they are resigned to just live out their lives together as companions, compatible in their differences. They treat each other formally and politely when humans are around, never going beyond a casual sniffing when the other passes by. But then when we're gone for the day, I know they sneak off and sleep together in the guest bedroom on the second floor.

Who am I to say that one way of finding God is better than another?

If You Lived Here

I Hope He's Happy Down There

I have a good friend whom I met at Divinity School a few years ago. He was a prosperous businessman, who in mid-life decided to become a minister. I thought at the time that he would probably make an extraordinary minister. He was strong, yet sensitive; passionate about his beliefs, yet understanding of others. He was also a dedicated Red Sox fan, which in a Boston suburb couldn't hurt. One thing about him that he doesn't talk about too much is that he is also "gay," that gentle euphemism some people use for being homosexual.

The first church he served was a large prosperous one in a Boston suburb. He got off to a fairly good start. Good sermons, good programs, good youth work. However, after a few months he decided that he should be honest and tell them about his controversial sexual orientation. I think he figured that since homosexuality is such an emotional, polarizing subject, it would be better to tell the truth than to continue being dishonest about himself and then someday be found out. In a sermon one Sunday he talked about the struggles, the secrecy, the ridicule, and the nasty looks he often got from people when they knew. He told it all.

I don't know how well the sermon was received with the congregation. Some time after that he was working with his sexton in the church's fellowship hall. They were changing light bulbs. My friend held the ladder while the sexton climbed it to reach the lights. When they finished, they both carried the ladder back to the storage closet. As I recall, they were talking about the sermon and my friend's homosexuality. The sexton was fairly quiet during the conversation, but by itself that didn't seem odd. But suddenly, without warning, the sexton rammed the ladder forward and pinned my friend's head against the wall. Then the sexton began hitting him and kicking him repeatedly until he finally fell to the ground. He remembers screaming but he couldn't get away. The sexton was a big man and he continued swinging his fists at my friend in rage until he finally was unconscious. He doesn't remember anything after that for some time, but he understands from the stories told by people who came in to stop the fight that the sexton continued hitting him again and again long after he was unconsciousness on the floor.

He was in the hospital for several days after that from broken bones, lacerations, and a serious concussion in his head. And he was in bed for several days more eating with a straw and trying to learn to walk again. When he finally returned to the church everyone tried to be very nice. The sexton was punished, the people forgave him, everyone was sympathetic, everything was back to normal, but not long after that my friend left the church. He moved away and took a tiny little church in a tiny town down along the Mexican border and so far as I know, that's where he is today.

I thought about him today because I've heard so many stories recently about churches firing ministers who were gay, or denominations de-churching local congregations when they hired someone who was gay. And, of course, our nation continues to debate whether it is right to allow homosexuals to serve their country in the military or hold office or buy property, or join major political parties. Maybe I have also remembered his story because it's hard to argue about "those people" in the abstract when I can remember my friend's face after he got out of the hospital.

I hope my friend is happy down there on the border. With his skills and gifts he could be an extraordinary minister. I wonder if he has gotten the courage to tell them the truth yet.

And Did You See Him Smile?

I read about my friend Ron Freeman in the paper last week. There he was, smiling up at me from the page and looking real fine. Ron always wanted to be famous.

It's no wonder fame was so important to him. To hear Ron tell it, his father spent half his life telling him how unimportant he was and how he'd never amount to anything. He once told me that the most important thing in his entire life was for him to do something that would make the whole country sit up and take notice. He even admitted that the only reason he ever went to college was to become a lawyer and run for office and eventually become president. There are worse reasons, I suppose.

That dream didn't make, however. When he was in college he and some friends took off up to Gatlinburg to go skiing, and on their way home Sunday night they hit another car. Ron was fine, but two of his friends died, and the mother and child in the other car died. Ron was driving. He was drunk. It was the third time he'd been stopped while being drunk. The judge gave him six months time in Brushy Mountain State Penitentiary.

That probably would have been the end of the story if he hadn't run off. But Ron said he couldn't stand it in a place like that and one day he just snuck off. It was amazingly easy. For one thing Ron didn't "look" like the stereotype of a prisoner. He was tall, blond-haired, and handsome. He looked like a college kid, or a young attorney off of the job. So, one day he saw a group of engineers and contractors going in and out of the gate, working on plans for a prison expansion. He put on a "free side" shirt, grabbed a clipboard, and walked toward the gate flipping pages and looking official. They let him walk on through.

After he got away, he got a job, changed his name (to "Freeman" because that's what he was now), got married, and settled down. He even joined a local Presbyterian church and taught Sunday school on occasion. That also might have been the end of it except that Ron still needed to be famous. As a free man he ran for the legislature and put his picture all over Knoxville and somebody recognized it. In the thick of the campaign he was arrested again. This time he was given seven years, and this time he was sent to the maximum security prison in Nashville.

When I met Ron there when I was working at the prison as a chaplain. He was still doing time and still trying to think of something he could do that would make him famous. He had just gotten married again to a woman he'd met in the prison visitation program, and was writing a book about his life. If people could just read about what had happened to him, he said, he could become famous for sure. People from all over the country might read his book and know about the plight of prisoners, and he might do some good with it and, of course, he might become a little famous in the process.

After a while, I moved back to Oklahoma and the prison authorities moved Ron back up to Brushy Mountain. That was terrible. It's a terrible place. It's far up in the mountains and his wife couldn't visit him very often. In the last letter I ever got from him, Ron said he wasn't sure he could last in such a place much longer. He said being in prison was wasting his life and there were important big things he should be doing out in the free world.

That's the last thing I ever heard about Ron until last week, when he had finally gotten himself famous. One day he and several other guys tied up a guard and broke out of Brushy Mountain. One turned himself in almost as soon as they got out. Three more were captured within a day or so. The two that were left got cornered in an abandoned house somewhere up in

Kentucky and the police shot their way in. After all the shooting was over, one of the two was captured; Ron was killed.

I wished, when I heard about it, that I had answered his last letter. I wished that I had said something to him that would have made him want to stay. I wished that years ago I could have convinced the judge that Ron wasn't really a criminal but just a guy that got in trouble. I wished a lot of things.

Oh well, maybe Ron is happy now, since he finally got himself famous. Maybe he finally got what he wanted, pictured up there in the television set, looking down at the rest of the world, looking at us with a smile.

If You Lived Here

Carl and Alice

"**I**t's good riddance to her anyway," he said. He walked down the hall like I wasn't there and stomped into the bedroom. "She wasn't worth being around in the first place so I'm just as glad to be going." He was carrying a bundle of shirts which he pushed down into a big canvass bag on the bed and pulled the string up tight on them. "Alice," he called out to no where in particular. "Where are our big suitcases? The ones I take on trips?" No answer.

"Carl," I said, trying to sound composed in the midst of his fury. "Maybe you and Alice could still sit down and talk this out."

"Forget it," he said, talking about suitcases and not my proposal. "I don't need them anyway." He stormed back down the hallway and into the kitchen. There he began pawing through the cabinets, finally finding a stack of paper grocery sacks under the sink. "Shopping Center Suitcases," he said, his face lighting up. "These are better than real suitcases anyway and there's always plenty of them."

Carl and Alice had always had a pretty spicy relationship. First one would blow up, and then the other. She would accuse him of not showing her enough affection, and then he would say that not only does he show her affection, but that he showed her more affection than she did. Or she'd say that he was too demanding, and then he'd say that he never demanded anything at all from her and that she was actually the overly demanding one. They did this kind of thing all the time. It was a joke at the church, that no matter what Alice would accuse Carl of, sooner or later he would accuse her of the same thing, only horrendously worse. Or it would be the other way around. However, through it all we all still believed that they loved each other and nothing would come of their petty bickering. That was just the way they related.

This day looked like it might be different. Alice called me this morning steaming and shouting that it had finally happened. She couldn't take it any more and she was actually, finally, leaving him. I rushed right over, but when I arrived Carl met me at the door. "She lied to you on the phone," he said. "She is not leaving me. She is a coward and would never do that. But the truth is I'm leaving her."

I didn't want to debate the matter. "Where is Alice now?" I said.

"Oh, she's back in the back of the house, crying her eyes out. She's worried that I'm leaving her and she's back there weeping like a little girl." I looked over his shoulder and couldn't hear anything but it was a big house and there were some rooms I didn't know anything about.

When he finished gathering up the grocery bags from the cabinet under the sink, he went back into the bedroom and began stuffing more clothing into the sacks. "Where's the cleaning, Alice? I need all of my clothes, y'know." She still didn't answer. "Stupid woman," he said. "Don't worry sweetheart," he said, sneering at the doorway. "I can pick them up later." He looked at me as though we were both in on this together. "Disgusting woman," he said.

He looked around the room for something else he might need to take with him. "How about the bedspread? That would get to her," he said. "Her Oh-So-Special bedspread, the hand-quilted gift from her great and glorious mother—the bedspread that no one was able to sit on and no one was able to put anything on." I was sitting on the bed when he said that and I didn't move.

"Carl, you really don't want to take this bedspread." I tried to sound firm.

"Naw," he said, "You're right. I'll leave it. I won't have a place for it anyway."

He went back to the closet again and pulled out a dirty cardboard box. It had old shoes, ties, paint, rusty tools, and a jar of nails in it that were being saved for a garage sale. "This is a good box," he said. "I can use this." He pulled it out into the bedroom and dumped it onto the bedspread.

"Carl!" I gasped.

"Good bedspread," he said.

He went back into the closet and came out with a drawer full of socks and underwear. It's her fault, y'know." He emptied the socks into the box. "Jesus, she could be cruel." He threw the empty drawer onto the floor. "Alice, is the rest of the laundry finished yet?" No answer. "I hate her," he said. "I really hate her."

He threw the other sacks into the box and lifted it to his shoulder. "I'm coming out now, Alice, so you're gonna have to look at me." He looked out cautiously into the living room. "Here I come." No sounds came from the living room. In fact, no sounds came from anywhere else in the house. I was wondering at this point if she had already gone. The kids, too, were no where to be seen. We both went out the front door to his car, which was all alone in the drive way. It didn't look like anyone was home at all.

"I'll bet she just took them and went down the street to the Coopers' after the fight," he said. "She's probably just afraid to see me when I'm like this, so she's hiding out and crying and is coming right back as soon as I'm out of here." He laughed. "I'm really gonna show her. I really am gonna be out of here. Then she'll really have something to cry about." He opened the trunk and set the box next to another similar box full of assorted tools and garden equipment. "We'll just see if she can trim the stupid hedge without these things," he said. Then he went back to the house and I followed him, feeling a little inconsequential in this whole ordeal. In the bedroom he grabbed another armload of sacks and boxes he had filled. "Last chance to say something nasty before its too late," he yelled into the emptiness. "This is good old Carl leaving you forever." No sounds from the rest of the house. He took the load out to the car.

"Carl," I said, standing in his driveway, "you suppose you ought to leave her a note, or something. I mean, just walking out like this, with no word between you...nothing?" I was flailing around trying to think of something to say. "That feels like a terrible thing to do."

He looked at me like I was child who didn't understand the complexity of his grand plans. "So, okay, I'll leave her a note." He laughed. "I'll write her a note to tell her to get screwed...and good riddance, and that I hate her."

"That wasn't what I had in mind."

He laughed again a wicked triumphant laugh and ran back into the house to look for a pencil and paper. He went in the kitchen and started looking though the drawers. He found a little stub of a pencil, but he couldn't find any paper. Surely there should be a scrap in there somewhere. He looked around the room but he couldn't see any paper anywhere. I had just joined him in the kitchen when he looked up and noticed a bright orange wooden clock on the wall by the refrigerator and his eyes grew large. "That was my mother's clock," he said. "She's got no right to it."

"Want me to help you get it? I asked.

"No, I got it." With one immoderate sweep of his hand, he reached up at it and jerked it off the wall. Plaster and paper came off with it.

I gasped again.

"Sorry Alice," he said, though he was smiling when he said it. He took the clock over to the cabinet, grabbed the pencil and went out through the kitchen to the garage to look for some paper. On a nail over his workbench was a clipboard and paper hanging on a nail. There's some, he smiled.

"Last chance, Sweetie Pie," he said through the door to the empty house. He opened the garage door and carried his clock, clipboard and pencil out to the car. "I'll leave the note behind for her here so she can see it when she comes back," he said to nobody in particular. By this time I might as well have been a part of the furniture. "She's really disgusting," he said, "walking out on me right after I told her I was getting ready to leave her."

He began scribbling on the paper but before he got a whole line out, his pencil lead broke. "Damn. That's my only pencil." He clawed at it with his fingernails to get another piece of lead out. "Ouch," he said. He had driven a splinter into his finger. "I hate these things." He put the pencil in his mouth and tore the first sheet off of the pad. He closed his eyes and thought hard about what he should say to her. He was fuming. His hands trembled. He laid the clipboard down for a minute and rubbed his hands together to get the nervousness out of them. He hit his chest several times to get himself to stop breathing so hard. He closed his eyes again. "Okay, here goes." He looked down at his paper. "This is going to be the last time I'll ever have to say anything to her again. From this point on it will all be through the attorneys. He liked the thought of that. "Dear Alice." He stopped and tore the sheet off.

"What happened? I asked.

"Forget the 'Dear.' She doesn't deserve a 'dear.'" He rubbed his hands together again. "Alice," he wrote. He looked hard at the word. "Go on," he said to himself, "finish it." He tightened his jaw and leaned down on his pad. He began writing furiously and pressed down so hard he broke through the paper twice. It seemed to take forever. But finally he was finished. "There," he said, looking at his words, "that's her." He pulled the car door shut and started up the motor. He thrust the clipboard into my hands and said, "Make sure she gets this."

"Where are you going?" I asked.

"Doesn't make any difference," he said. "I'm just going. You make sure she gets the note and that'll finish up everything." He backed the car out of the driveway, and pulled out into the street. "And *don't* read it," he said.

As he drove off, the pages of the clipboard crackled in the wind and I looked down at his words. I tried not to, but in spite of myself I read what he had written. It said, "Alice. I love you. I miss you and I am sorry. I hope you will forgive me and take me back again soon—Carl."

If You Lived Here

In My Father's House

February, 2005

On the eve of a vote by the US Congress to force doctors to keep alive a severely brain-damaged woman against the wishes of her husband.

Some years ago my step-father—at a time when we least expected it—had a stroke. He survived, and then with tremendous effort managed to carve out a diminished, but still productive, life for himself. But then he had another. And another. And another. Each one slowly draining him down to a level of being and existence he never imagined would happen to him. And then finally he had the last one. At first it didn't take his life, but it certainly took his soul.

I remember the night, weeks later, when we finally gathered around his bed in tears and torment for the meeting that every family dreads, and we discussed aloud for the first time whether we should let him go or keep him here, not wanting to admit that it was over. Our grief and fear was like a physical presence around us that we could feel and touch. That night we cried and prayed and hugged and looked deep into his eyes for a sign that there was something still there, still present, still hearing. But there was nothing. We could find only a deep and terrifying absence, an emptiness. The natural arc of his bodily functions was bending toward the end, and our love and memories were holding him back. The doctor, a friend of the family and a man of great faith himself, stood with us, about to lose an old friend, and he said that the future was in God's hands now and that he could do no more to help us. Some who had gathered there were doubters since childhood, but they held our hands, shared our words of faith, and felt with us the mystery of the presence of God in a way that can only come when one is overwhelmed with the horror of death.

We prayed for a wisdom that was larger and more profound than we in our weakness could envision on our own. We asked God whether and why and how this body should continue when the life in my father's eyes had grown vacant and cold.

And finally we made the decision, an awful, revulsive decision, to talk to the doctor and let my father go. To release his body to God and allow him finally to join the company of saints in everlasting peace. It was terrible, it was wrenching, and we've prayed continually since that time that we were right.

Today we look back on our decision that grueling, difficult night as a moment of sacred wonder. We stood frail and helpless at the door of death and touched the face of God. And in the process we felt loved, and held, and comforted. For us at that time and that place it was right to tell the doctor to 'let him go,' to let his body take its natural course, and I think, in the deep and everlasting mystery of life and beyond life, that my father somehow knows that, and agrees with us, and is glad.

And I also think how lucky we were. Not blessed, for that would be like God was playing favorites, but just lucky. We were just lucky to live in an age in which only a very few people could conceive that our personal painful decisions might be regulated by federal law. We were lucky that our difficult intimate choices were pushed onto us before we had a Congress that believed it right to tell families how and when to let their loved ones die with dignity.

And I pray that God will forgive us for allowing such madness to be promoted today in God's name.

Seeing and Believing

I hate to admit it, but more and more often these days, when I think about some of the more complex theological and political issues of the day, I am reminded of my cats.

For example, I've been stymied recently about the problem of why some people seem increasingly only able to believe in a God that they can see, hear, feel, and touch. I think the reason has something to do with our American "pragmatism" and the free market system. Pragmatism says that nothing exists unless you can hold in your hands and use it for something tangible and measurable. The market system says that nothing exists unless you can assign a price to it; *everything* has a monetary value and can be bought and sold. Unless you can buy it, sell it, hold it, put it in a showroom, it really doesn't exist. That growing philosophy (which wasn't there in the era of our grandparents) may be one of the reasons why today people are having a harder and harder time conceiving of even the *possibility* of God or the Holy Spirit.

This problem, of course, reminded me of our cat Geraldine. When Geraldine was very young there was a brief moment in time when she enjoyed chasing mice (admittedly she gave it up quickly because it was such an undignified task for a woman of leisure). But occasionally in her chasing, the mouse would run around to the backside of a door, and when that happened, she would immediately walk away because she could no longer see it. For Geraldine, the mouse didn't exist because it was no longer visible. We'd say, "Yo, Geraldine, don't quit looking! Don't give up believing that the mouse is there, just because you can't see it." But for Geraldine, seeing *was* believing, and since she couldn't see it, it didn't exist. So she'd flip her tail at us and head down the hall for a nap.

Our other cat, Mikey, on the other hand is the family mystic. She mysteriously "knows" when there is a mouse in the house. I don't know if she can hear it or smell it, or what, but somehow she can tell. One time last fall, when it was getting cold and we had problems with mice coming in from the woods, Mikey sensed one around suppertime. As she was just walking into the kitchen, she stopped suddenly, her hair stood up slightly, and her ears shot high. She knew somehow that something different was in the house. Quietly and carefully, she slinked over to the cabinet (where mice have been known to sneak in through the walls), and gently nudged at the door. We opened it and sure enough two surprised little beasts jumped up and scurried away. Now these days Mikey is too old to do much about mice when she finds them, but her powers of detection are still wonderful. Even in her old age, she has a remarkable gift of sensing the presence of something invisible but real that is undetectable to the rest of us.

I remember a made-for-TV movie a few years ago about the Loch Ness monster, starring Ted Dansen. There was a scene in the final part when Dansen, who played an American who had gone to Scotland to debunk the "Nessie" myth, told a young boy that he wanted to believe that it existed but he couldn't because he couldn't see it. He just had to see the creature before he could believe in it. The boy countered with a wisdom that almost religious. He said that Dansen had it all backward. "You mustn't try to see it first in order to believe in it," he said. "First you must believe in it, and then you can see it."

The little boy was exactly right, but at the same time, I don't know how I could base a church evangelism program on that truth. In this tortured, broken world, people are hungry for an encounter with the Holy, but they don't have the tools any longer to recognize the Divine unless they can see it, or hold in their hands, or buy it from a drugstore. How can they understand that they must *know* something before they can *see* it? Or that they must believe *in* God before they can believe *that* God exists?

Most of us are like Thomas, to whom Jesus said, Blessed are those who believe after seeing, but more blessed are those who believe without seeing.

Geraldine herself is not totally against getting excited over "the conviction of things not seen," as the Apostle Paul put it. Shortly after Mikey had discovered the mouse in the cabinet, Geraldine also came into the kitchen and she, too, sensed something was different in the room and she too grew excited. She pulled her ears back, her hair tensed up, and she stalked steadily and slowly across the room to the opposite wall. There, crouching against the cabinet, was her food dish and she pounced upon it, swallowing down a pound and a half of her geriatric-mix cat food. She knows her priorities.

And God also blesses those of us who only believe when the Holy Spirit is on *this* side of the door.

If You Lived Here

After a While It Will Become True

There's an interesting scene in John Steinbeck's epic novel *East of Eden*, that I wanted to tell you about. It takes place when an innocent young man named Adam Trask falls in love with a beautiful but truly evil woman named Cathy, who uses him and leaves him. She actually despised him from the start, but needs him because her employer (and lover) discovered her stealing from the brothel where she worked and beat her nearly to death. In the process of nursing Cathy back to health, Adam falls in love with her and eventually proposes to her, and because she still needs his home as a refuge, she says Yes. They do in fact marry and she even becomes pregnant, though it is unclear that it is because of Adam. When she finally gives birth to twin boys, Adam is ecstatic, but she announces that she is leaving him. When he tries to stop her, she coldly shoots him with his own gun and then walks calmly over his bleeding body and out the door.

He doesn't die, but he wishes that he had. For months Adam lives a less than lifeless existence. He is unable to move or think or talk. He ignores himself and his home and leaves the yet-to-be named twins in the care of a Chinese cook. Finally a wise neighbor named Samuel hears what is happening and comes to talk some sense into him. His advice to Adam sounds trite, but it is subtly profound. He looks Adam in the eye and tells him simply to "go through the motions." When Adam doesn't get it, he repeats, "Go through the motions. Act out being alive, like a play. And after a while, a long while, it will be true."

It does in fact take Adam a long time to hear and understand those words, but when he does, he begins to recover from the depths of his depression, and he does so because he has been able to "go through the motions" of being alive.

Those words haunted me some years ago when, for different reasons— divorce, job crisis, family deaths—I was going through my own bouts with depression. Daily life had become heavy and oppressive for me and it became difficult to even get up and move and function each day.

But even though I couldn't change the emotionally draining circumstances of my life, simply being forced to "go through the motions" of being alive contributed immensely toward eventually making it feel true.

As the pastor of a church, there was something empowering and redemptive about continually being forced to say the words of life to others while my own life was feeling so lifeless. Eventually I found myself unable to remain feeling "dead" while being in the midst of these words which promised so much life. One cannot easily stand before the gathered fellowship week after week repeating the words of the assurance of pardon, and lifting up the body of Christ, "broken for you" (and for me), without eventually feeling the power of their redemptive mystery. Even words repeated meaninglessly will eventually take meaning. Words of forgiveness and redemption, repeated again and again even by rote, eventually becomes real, despite our (my) strongest inclinations to keep them otherwise. Say the words, said Samuel to Adam, "act out being alive...and after a while, a long while, it will be true."

William Willimon, the former chaplain at Duke University, tells a story of the day a Greek Orthodox priest lectured a class on the meaning of the historic creeds. During the question period, one of the students asked the Priest how he, the student, could say the creeds when there were parts of them he didn't believe in. The priest said to just keep repeating them. Eventually they will come to you. But the young man came back several times plaintively saying he simply didn't *believe* them and therefore he *couldn't* say them. The priest, obviously frustrated, finally said something like "But they are not your creeds to believe or disbelieve. They belong to the church and to history. There are many things that you cannot believe at your age. Just keep saying them. Eventually the meanings of them will come to you. Just keep saying them, and eventually the truth that is in them will come to you, and you will believe them."

What that means, I think, is that some of the most important truths of our lives come to us not from our minds but from our lives. They come not through our ears but through our motions. It also means that those people who act as though the kingdom or realm of God has already arrived, do in a mysterious way already live within it. When you *do* the deeds of God's realm—things like feeding the hungry, healing the sick, comforting the lonely, sheltering the homeless, liberating the oppressed—then for you the realm of God will have arrived.

The message, I think, is to do it. Go through the motions. Act like you are truly alive; act like God truly is in control of your life and the world. It may not be so now. It may feel false right now. But do it anyway, and "after a while...it will be true."

If You Lived Here

A Whole Lot More

Out on the highway, out by Hontubby,
there usta live an old fella named John Bails
who got in trouble with the law here
few years back.
Ol John was a mean kid when he was young,
fightin' alla time. We never thought
he'd amount to much of anythin'.
Got hisself all busted up and throwed
in jail mor'n once and
we all thought he'd get hisself kilt one a these days.
Ran off two wives before he ever straightened out,
an' had mor'n that live with 'im off 'n on.

But ol John seemed to pull hisself up after that.
He got religion, he said. That's what did it.
What happened was he nearly died a bleedin' one time
after a fight he got into out back a the Eagles Lodge.
Two boys accused John of messin' around with his wife.
John dint do it, but theys both too drunk to know better,
    and so they beat 'im terrible regardless

and then they threw him inta the dumpster in the alley.
John laid there for more'n two days bleedin' an' hurtin'
before someone come by to empty the trash and found him.
He said th' only thing what kept him alive them two days was
seein' the face a Jesus inside that dumpster
tryin' to comfort him, and reachin' down and touchin'
John's wounds to make 'em not feel so bad.

He even started doin' some preachin' after that happened,
up there in one a them churches out by th' Black Fork River.
And from what we heard, he did real good at it too.
Brought a lotta folks inta church what never
woulda done it 'cept for a way he had about him
ever since he become a believer hisself.
There wern't nobody what had a gooder heart
than ol John after that an' there wern't a person
in this area what din't think th' most of 'im.
Used to preach against all that fightin'
          he hisself used to do.
Said that if you really had your heart in the right place,
you din't need to get messed up with all that.
Yessir, John sure had a way about 'im after that.

He raised hisself up a good sized boy, too.
One he got offa that first wife what run off.
They both just lived out there in the woods
tryin' to make a livin' pullin' in trees
          for the charcoal plant.
We all never seed how he could make enough money
to keep even hisself alive, let alone that big ol boy.

But they seemed to do all right, although
they lived in the sorriest place you ever saw.
Was a ratty old thing he built hisself
what was cold in the winter

and hotter'n blazes in the summer.
It was snug back up inta the forest,
with just enough trees cleared so he could raise
a few potatoes, an' tomatoes, an' some beans.
He din't never seem to complain about it though.
John just said the lilies of the field never
had any bettern that, so's its all right wi' him.

Ol John took real good to that boy a his too.
Said one time that watchin' that boy grow up's
what give 'im his faith.
I s'pose that could be true when he was just a little'n,
but after he growed up some we couldn't figger it.
Specially seens how that boy a his was a whole lot more
of a handful than his papa ever was.
He stayed drunk 'bout alla time and one time or 'nother
stole a thing or two from about alla us.
We all knew it but John never could see it.
I think a fellow sometimes goes a little
blind when he's talkin' 'bout his own kid.
Specially if it's his only one and he's got
no wife or anybody to tell 'im
how he don't know what he's talkin' about.
We all thought a awful lot a John
and knowed how much he thought a that boy,
so we never said anythin' to 'im about it.
But the boy still wern't worth nothin', regardless.

One time that boy a his come inta town
yellin' to everyone about how he's gonna
        get back at Billy Murrow
for takin' some girl a his away from him.
We din't pay no attention to him but we heard later on
how he'd gone and busted out all th' windows
        of Billy's daddy's OTASCO store and

broke up a bunch a stuff on th' inside an' even
broke the cash register when he
found there wern't no money in it.

We knowed there was trouble then,
so we closed up th' station and drove out to Hontubby
to see if John had heard about all this here yet.
When we got there Billy Murrow'd already been there
        an' left.
Billy'd wanted to just demand money for the damages,
but they both got ta arguin' an' fightin'
and Billy got his daddy's deer rifle from his pickup
and he fired it.
He pret'near shot John's boy's face off with the rifle.
He wern't dead yet when we got there,
        but we was fixin' to,
        we could tell.

John was goin' crazy.
He'd just walked up from the charcoal plant
and seen Billy Murrow drive off.
He knew just exactly what had happened.
We tried to hold 'im down some
but he just kept throwin' us off
and hollerin' that there wern't no God
        and there wern't no Heaven
        and that nothin'd do but for him to go into town
        and find Billy Murrow and to beat his brains out.

He finally did run off from us,
and he took his own rifle with him,
but we figured we hide th' keys to th' car an' he couldn't
go too far outen th' woods without 'em.
So we decided to sit an' wait for 'im there,
that maybe he'd run down after a while

an come on back inside.
We din't figure that one right, though,
'cause it wern't no mor'n an hour before we got word
he'd run all th' way back to town
and found Billy Murrow drinkin' beer at th' Eagle Lodge.
They said John din't say nothin' to 'im at all.
He just walked up real fast behind him
and stuck his own gun in Billy's back,
and blew a hole through him.

* * * * *

We all never saw much a John after that.
Billy Murrow survived though he couldn't get around much.
He'd lost a chunk of his lung and a
whole bunch a bones on his rib cage.
We all figured John coulda gotten off on one a them
"temporary insanity" type things, but from what
we heard, John never tried to plead nothin'.
Just sat there through the whole trial lookin' stupid.
Th' courts give 'im a lawyer from up in Poteau,
but they never said much to one another.
John really never had much of a chance,
but then he never wanted one neither.

After the trial they took 'im off over there to
that prison in McAlester for a couple a years,
but finally they sent 'im on home.
They knew he wern't no killer.
Just a fella what loved his son too much;
so much it drove 'im a little blind or crazy or both,
an made 'im forget everthin' he ever taught us folks
about hurtin' and killin'.

Folks here never knew what to think of ol John

after all that happened.
Din't know whether to trust 'im
or believe in him or nothin'.

He never come inta town much again
to see the rest of us neither.
Just stayed out in that sorry old house a his,
sittin' there on th' porch lookin' outen th' forest.
I went out by there a few times since all this here happened
and ast 'im if he'd wanta go with us to do this or that
but he never would.
He'd just sit there lookin' terrible.
He'd always look like he was just gittin' ready to cry.
But he never did cried.
So far's I know.
I never seen 'im cry.

He'd wait there until
I'd decide to go on an' leave 'im alone.
He never did much a anythin' after that,
'sides sittin' on that porch an lookin' off into that forest.
That an' hurt.
He did a lot a hurtin'.

I 'spose he did a whole lot more a that
than he ever did before in his life.

Where Is God in This Process?

"Where is God in this process?" That's what a new pastor asked me after standing in for me in taking Communion to a local nursing home while I was out of town. He was appalled, or perhaps stricken, at the sense of hopelessness of the residents. They (many, at least) could barely raise their heads, they seemed to be not aware of the "show" going on in front of them. They seldom responded. They were wheeled back and forth helplessly by distracted orderlies. Where is God in this process?

Should we continue ministering to a gathering of strangers who seem not aware of their neighborhood, and are unable to come out and play in it? Is God present, absent, uninvolved, bored?

Years ago my wife, who is also a pastor, did her ministerial field placement at the Fernald State School in Waltham, Massachusetts. She was assigned to the Catholic priest there because the staff figured one religion's as good as another and "we're all going to the same place anyway," whatever that means. Father Henry Marquardt was the mysterious renegade priest whom God sent to be her supervisor. He not only let her preach in the Mass, but also allowed her (at that time a Unitarian) to assist with the sacraments. The clients called her "Father Beverly."

If You Lived Here

Once a month he would take the Eucharist to the hinterlands, the severely retarded quarters where lived the residents who seldom gave apparent notice of being present. Henry would do the entire liturgy with ecstasy, buoyancy, constantly touching, hugging, and generally reveling in the joy of being in their grimly maintained company. Crossed eyes crusted over with dry sleep and tears would watch him rapturously. Slobber sealed smiles would break out in glee for the first time in weeks. Bodies filled with absence would rouse and applaud with palms and elbows and wrists and whatever could be slapped together in celebration. The nurses told me once, while I watched his being amazing, that no drug, food, therapy, or needle that they had ever seen or heard of could go so far toward bringing the clients back home again as Henry Marquardt singing and dancing the praises of the body and blood of Jesus Christ.

Where was God in the process? I remember my mother back in Oklahoma anguishing over her father and my grandfather during his last years, which were terrorized by Alzheimer's. Should she continue reading to him, she asked, even when he called her "Bill" and talked about a spring planting of wheat in the room next door? Is there any way that he could know and experience the joys of the saving presence of Jesus Christ, our Rock and our Redeemer, from within his mighty fortress of memorylessness?

Do you remember the movie "Awakenings" with Robin Williams playing the neurologist Oliver Sacks in his first job in a hospital in the 1950s? In it Sacks stumbles across a treatment which brings nearly-comatose patients back to consciousness again (temporarily) and for a while they rediscover life in all its joys and sorrows. One of them who came back from a long and deep darkness was Robert DeNiro, who gets a crush on a young woman who comes weekly to the hospital to read to her grandfather. She doesn't know that DeNiro is a patient and so they become friends. After some visits, she tells him that she is not sure that she will continue reading to her grandfather because he never responds. She no longer thinks he can hear her; perhaps she should just stop. When they part and DeNiro is walking away, a thought comes to him. He turns back to her and says, "Don't stop reading to your Grandfather. He hears you. He hears you."

Is God in the process, or is God the voice in the Absence? My son nearly died one night years ago from an asthma attack. We were out in the country, an hour's drive to a hospital. He was so swollen and weakened that he couldn't hear us when we spoke to him. We kept him alive by rubbing his tummy in the car seat on the way to the doctors. Once when I thought he'd fallen unconscious, I stopped rubbing and began using my hands to talk and point out directions to my wife who was driving. From somewhere far away in his consciouslessness, Stanley reached up and put my hand back on his tummy. He had been listening intently to my non-words and wanted them to continue.

Don't ever stop reading to Grandfather, Mom.

If You Live Here

Redemption

Years ago, right after I graduated from divinity school, I worked for a while as a chaplain at a small rural prison known as "Camp Hodgens." I didn't really want the job. It was during a very dry season for me spiritually and, for a time there I was actually considering leaving the ministry. But some friends talked me into taking the job while they searched for a permanent chaplain.

While there, I got acquainted with an inmate named Billy Kioga. In addition to being a prisoner, he was also a husband, a carpenter, and an alcoholic dying from cirrhosis of the liver and a bleeding stomach. He was there because he had received six "DUIs" in a row, and a Judge decided to show off his considerable ignorance of the disease of alcoholism by sending Billy to prison for a couple of years to "cure" him. I guess he thought that Billy's overwhelming criminal mind was what caused him to drink and that losing his job, being separated from his family, and sitting in prison making license plates would stop him from being so rotten.

We became friends because we both came from dirt-farmer families and town-drunk fathers. I actually felt pretty awkward around him but I tried to not let on. Billy was twice my size with big heavy hands callused up from swinging hammers and saws for a living. Sometimes he would get so mad at something—his room, Camp Hodgens, his wife, whatever—that he would swing one of those meaty hands down on a table or the side of his bed and the whole room would shake. He didn't have a reputation for violence, at least not while he was in the camp, but on occasion he looked like he had it in him, and I never was sure if I might set him off. If Billy would ever swing one of those huge hands at someone, he could kill him.

I think Billy knew that he was dying and why, but he didn't know how to do what he needed to do to stop it. He asked me on occasion to pray for him, but my prayer life was pretty barren in those days, so I said religious words to him instead, but that seemed to help. Sometimes, when people are as low as he was even a rope, without a boat hooked onto it feels like a rescue.

About two months before his parole, he got a letter from his wife up in Tulsa, which said in essence that while he'd been away things had gone from bad to worse and that she'd moved the family back to Tucson. Then just before his "quit time" came, he got another letter from her attorney suing him for divorce. It was the worst thing that could have happened. He tried to act like it didn't matter, because that was what men are "supposed" to act like, but everybody knew it broke him. The day he got out he went into town and got so drunk that he went crazy. About midnight he ran out of money and had the manager of the bar give me a call. The manager thought it was a call to me to bring more money, but it wasn't. Evidently, after he called, Billy went into the bathroom, broke the mirror off of the wall, and drove a huge chunk of it into his chest trying to cut out his stomach I suspect he was trying to get to his liver.

When I arrived they pushed me into the bathroom with him and closed the door. He was lying in the floor by the sink, dying. They wrapped him up the best they could, and called the emergency room at the Indian Hospital over in Talihina, but that was an hour's drive away in Ft. Smith, and it didn't look like he would make it.

I stood in the door for several minutes, shaking. I wanted to leave more than anything else in the world because I knew I didn't have anything at all to say to him or to give him. He finally looked up at me and smiled.

"I don't feel very good," he said quietly.

"Why'd you do it, Billy?" I asked.

"I don't know. I guess I thought they'd stop me."

"Can I get you anything?"

"No," he said. "But if you can just sit here for a while, I'd appreciate it.

I sat down next to him and put his head in my lap and leaned against the door of a toilet stall. We didn't speak for a few minutes more, and I began to cry. Not so much for my friend's suffering, I think, as for my own inadequacy to speak to him. I didn't have anything to say to him or to give him that could help him. I wanted to just leave him and run, but the pain of leaving was worse than the pain of staying, so I sat there, holding his head and after a time we talked. He talked about his life with Sally, his wife, and all the lies and deceit and drinking that had ruined their marriage. He said that he had taken her for granted at the time but now it had all finally come back on him and now she could no longer stand him. He deserved what he got from her, he said. It wasn't right, what he did.

His remorse was genuine, I think, but now it was too late. Now in his stupor, there seemed no other way to atone for his guilt than to gouge out the offending source of all his evil. He asked me to pray for him again and I tried and failed again but, as before, he said he felt better. In fact we both felt better.

We sat together on the floor for more than an hour after that, sometimes talking, sometimes crying, and sometimes trying to pray. In the calm, with two sons of dirt-farmers and town-drunks holding on to each other feeling lost for very different reasons, we both finally began to feel relaxed, maybe healed, perhaps forgiven; and then he died.

If You Lived Here

Snake Handlers

John and Mary were a nice young couple who used to be very active in the church. I liked them both a lot, though I knew Mary better than John because she dropped by the church more often during the daytime and we would talk. John had an interesting job training snakes to perform in the circus, and Mary was able to buy a big house in the country with the money he made from selling the snakes. But Mary also did a lot of complaining to the neighbors about how bad the snakes were to have around her nice house. She said they ate the furniture and ruined the carpet, and she constantly had to be running out and buying new things to go in the house.

John, on the other hand, denied it all. He said that the snakes ate mice and small animals, not furniture, and he said that someone else—the kids or the neighbors or somebody—was simply stealing different pieces of the furniture. And besides she shouldn't be talking about him to the neighbors behind his back.

She also complained a lot to her women's group at the church. She complained that the snakes were terrible and ugly and that he kept them in the house just to spite her because he didn't like her mother. On the other hand, John insisted that there was nothing wrong with having snakes around the house and that she was just saying all that to make people not like him because he didn't go to church too much. She used to break down during the sharing time at the women's Bible study and tell all the women about her problems with the snakes. She usually had a good cry, got it all off her chest, received a lot of good sympathy from the ladies, and then went home feeling a whole lot better. But after a few months of this, I figured things were getting out of hand, and it was probably about time I went by to see them.

They both seemed to be doing fine when I got there. We all three chatted pleasantly while Mary served us coffee on the new coffee table she had just purchased with money John had made selling the snakes. I noticed, however, some time into the evening, that old John was having a little trouble holding his coffee cup, and then I realized that his right hand was missing. It looked like it had been bitten off right up past his wrist and all that was left was a stub. I asked him about it. I said, "John, what happened there to your hand?" I said, "You never told me you lost a hand."

John said, "Oh, it's been gone a long time," he said. "I think I lost it in the war."

Mary sniffed up her nose and looked away. "The snake bit it off," she said. And looked valiantly the other way.

John said, "It ain't so. I lost it in the war," and he reached over and punched her out with his stub.

About a month or so later I saw Mary again at the furniture section down at Sears. I asked her how things were going and she said fine, smiling real brightly. But I noticed that she was also crying while she was smiling, so I asked her if something was really wrong.

"Well," she said, "One a them snakes ate up little Johnny Jr. last week and I just haven't quite gotten over it yet."

"Little Johnny!" I said. "That's terrible. You must be feeling awful."

"Well, it's been bad," she said. "But the ladies at the church have come by with food and all, and besides I got a chance to show off some of my new furniture (that we got from John selling them snakes) to everyone who came to the funeral and I had a good cry and got it all off my chest, and I'm feeling a lot better now."

"Have you ever though about getting rid of the snakes" I said?

70

"Oh, yes, they're terrible and all," she said. "They eat up things and make a mess and you know, you constantly have to be buying new things to replace them with? And by the way did I tell you that I'm pregnant again? We're going to get us a new baby, and John and I are so happy."

I gasped. "Yes, but what about the snakes?"

She sniffed and looked away again. "Well," she said, "we certainly can't afford to get rid of the snakes now. We need the money too badly. After all, how could we ever afford to buy all of these nice things for the house and the new baby if John didn't sell snakes?" She turned and walked off angrily. I was trying to think of something to say when she turned back and said, "You know, I would have called the church office about the funeral, but I only wanted to tell people I thought would be sympathetic to my problem." I gasped again.

The last I ever heard about John and Mary they were filing for a divorce. John had lost his whole arm by then and Mary had lost part of her foot. John said he was leaving Mary because she talked about him behind his back. Mary said she was leaving John because he didn't like her mother. He got the new baby and she got the house. Last I heard they were still fighting over who got to keep the snakes.

If You Live Here

Used Cars and Donuts

When my uncle passed away some years ago, I inherited his old 1962 Plymouth Satellite, you know, the ones that were a block long, foot-tall fins, and push-button transmissions. It was a great old car with only about eighty-thousand miles on it, and it ran better than the car I have now, which isn't nearly that old. I saw it for the first time when I was down at his home in Norphlet, Arkansas (population 300), for his funeral. His sister, who took care of him after he had gotten old and ill, was going down a list for me of all of his possessions and she mentioned the car. "Of course," she added, "you'll have to get it inspected if you want to drive it much."

"When was it inspected last?" I asked her.

She thought for a moment. "Early '70s, I would guess. Maybe longer."

She was right. I took the car over to nearby Eldorado, (Norphlet didn't have its own service station), and the attendant was stunned. "Nineteen seventy-one," he said, letting out a long whistle. "That's a Federal crime, y'know."

I knew that. But what I didn't know was why my uncle had let it go for so long. When I got back I asked my aunt how it was he never got it inspected, and she said it was because the parking brake was broke and he was afraid it wouldn't pass inspection.

"Why didn't he just fix the brake?"

"Well," she said, "he'd been planning to for a long time, but I guess he just never got around to it. You know how things slip by."

"But that was about twenty years. How did he sneak by that long without ever getting caught?"

"Since you mentioned it, I don't know if I remember him ever driving the car all that much anyway. He was afraid the county sheriff would see him and give him a ticket."

"Wait a minute," I said. "So how did he get around town without a car, if he was so afraid of getting caught without a sticker since it wouldn't pass the inspection for his brakes that didn't work?"

She looked at me like I was from another planet and didn't have a clue as to how the earth worked. "You know, people can learn to get by and do just about anything if they have a mind to. Your uncle learnt to be just real creative in that regard."

A couple of Sunday mornings ago I was in a donut shop in Duxbury, Massachusetts, reading the paper and I got into a conversation with an interesting fellow who was a retired postman in the area and who eats breakfast there every morning. He was a big fellow with a long mustache, who loved to eat jelly donuts with powder all over them. While we ate we made some small talk about our jobs and our families. After I told him about my own family, I asked if he was married. He said yes he was. A wife and three kids. Since I didn't see them anyplace, I asked if they were out of town.

Nope, he said, they were probably home right now getting ready for church.

I didn't want to pry, but that sounded odd. So I asked him kind of cautiously how it happened that he was here talking to me rather than back at home helping out with the kids?

"Well," he said, "The wife and me, we don't get along all that well." He took a big bite out of his jelly donut and swallowed some coffee. "So I just stay out of her way most of the time."

"That doesn't sound very pleasant," I said. "How long's this been going on?"

"Oh," he said, "about eighteen years."

74

"Eighteen years? How have you survived? Don't you miss the kids?"

"Oh," he said, "I miss them a lot, especially that little one. And I get real lonely on occasion. But I get by. One of these days I figure I'll drop by for a good visit and make amends for being away all this time." He rubbed a paper napkin over his mustache which had grown white with donut powder. "In fact, y'know, my doctor just told me that my health's not all that good, and it's possible that if I don't get over there sometime soon I might not be able to ever see them again before I go. So one of these days I figure I oughta get around to doing just that very thing." He looked at his watch and started folding up his paper. "I sure miss 'em, and it sure would be good to be around them now and then. But I've learned how to get real creative about filling up my time and getting along without them. One of these days I'll just go right on over there and things will be fine again."

We both paid for our donuts and coffee and left. But as I was driving away I thought about this guy and my uncle's Plymouth Satellite. I wondered to myself how often we use up our creativity coping with bad situations that we created trying to avoid creating bad situations? Maybe sometimes our fear of conflict actually winds up creating more conflict. Hmmm. I was also wondering if I ought to go back and see if he was interested in buying my used car.

If You Lived Here

76

Dog Story

That reminds me of a family I used to know who lived out by Lake Wister, on Fanny Creek. Larry and Martha were good folks who had a cute little girl named Amy and went to our church on Sundays.

When Amy turned 8, Martha bought her a little Doberman pinscher pup for a pet. Amy loved it. She used to hold it and hug it and wanted to take it with her wherever she went. We all thought they looked cute together and didn't see any harm in it.

Larry, on the other hand, saw red whenever saw the two of them together and didn't like that dog at all. "All Dobermans are killers," he told Amy when he was forbidding her to play with the dog. "I'm doing this for your own good."

I asked Larry about it one time. I said, "he doesn't look so bad to the rest of us, Larry, so why do you hate the dog?

He said, "That dog's a killer. All Dobermans are killers. I've had experiences with them, so I know. When he grows up he'll show his true colors."

We all heard stories about him hurting the dog and throwing things at him now and then, but most of us didn't pay much attention to it. However, a few months later I heard that when Amy was in Sunday school

Class, she started crying, saying how her Daddy had been beating her dog, and had penned him up in a tiny little cage in the backyard, and how she even thought that he had been secretly poisoning the dog food to kill him. I figured by this time that things were getting out of hand, so I went by to see what was going on. When I got over there, I found Larry out in back of the house working in the shed. I said, "Larry, what's the story between you and this here dog?"

He said, "It's not me; the dog's a killer and he tried to hurt Amy and I'm gonna stop him no matter what it takes."

I looked down at the dog and sure enough he was beginning to look pretty awful. He had a big gash on his face and several scars on his back where Larry had poured hot charcoal on him one time. He had a vicious, ugly look in his eye that I hadn't remembered seeing before. While we talked he snarled with rage at Larry. I could tell he had learned to hate Larry much worse than I had ever thought possible, based on what he'd looked like as a cute little pup just a few months before.

I started to say something, but I knew Larry wouldn't listen to it. He was already convinced that the dog was born rotten and always would be rotten, and nothing I could say about it would ever change him. About that time Larry chucked a two-by-four at the dog hitting him on his right hind leg. That must've done it. The dog let out a yelp and then lunged for all he was worth at the fence we were leaning on. He caught Larry by the collar bone and brought both of us and the fence all down on top of him. Larry was screaming and writhing around in the pen with the dog hanging onto his neck and clawing at his face and chest. I tried to get away, but I was caught in the fence and underneath both of them. Larry rolled back and forth and finally pulled himself over to the edge of the pen where he kept his tools. He made a terrible scream and swung his hand over into the box of tools. After a moment of searching in the box, he swung back again with a pair of pruning shears and drove them up into the rib cage of the dog. Blood went everywhere. The dog jumped straight up into the air and let out a loud howl and then fell four feet away from us limp.

A few days after that I stopped by the hospital to see Larry and to see how he was doing.

"How are you doing?" I asked him.

"Great," he said, "Just great. Finally we're safe in our home again. Nobody ever believed me about that dog and now they know he was a killer, just like I told 'em. He sure was a killer, wasn't he? Now at last we're safe."

If You Lived Here

Good Bye

Whenever you experience a personal loss you learn how much people care about you by the way they send condolences and cards. I think people feel a little bit of your own loss because it reminds them of pains that they have had over their own lives.

That was probably even true for the time when we finally lost our sweet little obese cat, Geraldine. She died quietly and nobly one night, just like she lived, and we still miss her fuzzy, stoic commentary on our stressed, overworked lives.

We always thought that Mikey would be the one to go first. Mikey cries and wails at her arthritis and various infections, but Geraldine was the brick, never complaining, never allowing herself to act in any way undignified. She would complain mightily about the absence of an abundance of food, but never about her health or wellbeing. She had her priorities.

Even at the end, during an awful night which followed awful days of being so sick that she couldn't even eat, when the pain of the tumor was taking an unbearable toll on her, she lay quietly in the hall by herself in her suffering. We could on occasion hear her moan, but we couldn't help her. My wife and I laid together on our backs in bed that night, holding hands and stared into the dark, crying over our own helplessness to tell her, or help her, or change what was hurting her. The mystery of death isn't any more clear or understandable for pets than it is for humans. At least with a human you can speak of a "better place." For Geraldine, life with her family is the better place. How could she think of going anywhere else?

The next day we took her to the vet and helped her the best way we knew how. Which means we held her, and lied to her, while a nice woman in a white coat and a gentle smile, came into the room and slowly took her life away from her. We petted her, and spoke to her, and watched her die. And then we went home.

I don't think she ever knew how famous she was. Friends of ours who read about her in my articles in the local paper would come by to visit on occasion, and when we would greet them at the door they would say, "Yes, hi, but first introduce me to Geraldine." We even got letters from strangers who read about her escapades with Mikey and her theological reflections on work and gardening. When she died, several of her fans sent us cards and money. I felt like I owed all of them one more Geraldine story to close the book. Mikey is also not doing all that well. Both of them are/were in their late teens, and soon we will have to close the book on her story as well.

But the last thing to say about Geraldine is that just as she took life well, she now has left it well, and now our house is one "person" less full. Not having grown up with cats I didn't know that someone could actually be a friend to such a lowlife creature as a cat. I thought God made them only for comic relief. Recently I ran across the stack of joke books I'd bought over the years and several of them were about cats. One was entitled, *Fifty Things to Do With a Dead Cat*. I felt ashamed and put it away. Geraldine deserved better. In her funny, fuzzy way, she taught me to be better. There is no such thing as a lowlife creature. No such thing as a creature created to be laughed at. God creates mysteries, God creates meaning. We are the ones who invent ridicule and disdain.

So, we miss her mightily; the old maiden aunt who lived with us and warmed our feet at night, and inspired us to love. In the end she was indeed a family member; she was indeed a friend.

Wonderful World

December, 2002

I got a call from a cousin in Oklahoma saying that my mother had fallen and was in the hospital. The doctors said she would survive, but should not live by herself in her home again. So, in the next two weeks I flew home, helped put her into an assisted living center, sell her home, and then held an estate sale of all of her household goods.

It was a bittersweet occasion. She is much better where she is now. She feels better, receives care, and is meeting friends. But we both grieved the loss of the home. Most of my childhood memories went out the door to strangers that week, paying ten cents on the dollar for every item regardless of how special it had once been to our family. All of our family paintings, gifts from friends, knickknacks from vacations went away. And even the piano went, which I had played for hours at a time when I was young, learning everything I know today about prayer and meditation and about music's mysterious kinship with the Holy Spirit.

The last day that I was there, when all of the crowds had left and our helpers had gone home, I cleaned and swept and hauled the trash, and tried to make the old house as pretty as I could so that it would look nice and proper and impress its new family. When I finally finished up I couldn't quite bring myself to leave, so I walked around the place, room by room, saying good-bye one last time. As I did, a small radio I was taking with me, that I had found in my mother's closet, began playing the old Louis Armstrong song, "It's a Wonderful World." It seemed a fitting piece to celebrate a home that had been both good and bad, beautiful and ugly, but overall a glorious part of a wonderful world.

I see trees of green, red roses too.

I see them bloom for me and for you.

And I think to myself, it's a wonderful world."

I flipped off the light in the living room and passed by the spot where my childhood piano had been just days before, and I saw a younger me sitting there painfully struggling to play Louis' song some forty years ago. I never could get the chords right. I walked from there into the den and saw all of my family still in their prime, watching a ball game after a Thanksgiving dinner and standing by the hearth with eggnog in hand, singing Christmas carols. In the kitchen my mother was preparing Easter lunch, in the back my dad was mowing the lawn, in the garage my brother, young and skinny, was fixing his car. Our dog, Buffy, still a puppy, wagged and barked and was glad to see me. She still looked the same after all these years.

I went through the garage and out to the car, and I stood in the driveway for a long while taking pictures of the house and listening to Louis sing its praises on my little radio. I thought what a marvelous gift that old house had been to all of us. I've loved it over the years. And I think in its own way it loved me back. It gave us warmth and peace and a sense of place. No matter how unhooked and far-flung my life would eventually become, the house was always there to come back to. It had a sacred comfort to it and a familiarity that I will never know again.

I see skies of blue, clouds of white.

Bright blessed days, dark sacred night,

And I think to myself, it's a wonderful world.

My memories there, both good and bad, help me see what kind of wonderful world we all live in. Closing down my old world there and returning to my new world here, I thought of the same comfort and companionship I feel now in my old white steepled New England church, lodged on this spot for almost three hundred years. This church building and its family seem cradled in the very love of God. People have been birthed here, warmed here, and challenged here for dozens of generations. I see them come and go, and some come back in their eighties and say, "I remember when I sang there in the children's choir." Or "I remember when we first installed that steeple." And no matter how unhooked or far-flung they've become, the love of God through Jesus Christ is always here. It will always continue to bless, inspire, empower, and redeem future generations for ministry and mission.

As I got in my car and turned on the ignition, Louis and I said good-bye one last time to the home where I once lived and moved and had my being. I'll be forever grateful for it, I thought. I thanked God for it. *I hear babies cry*, Louis was singing, *I watch them grow. They'll learn much more than I'll ever know.* And I thought to myself, it is in fact a very, very wonderful world.

If You Lived Here

Warmth in the Cold Places

Thanksgiving, 2002

This year my wife and I celebrated Thanksgiving with her family coming over to visit. My own family is scattered over four states and the District of Columbia, so we seldom see them all together in the same place. Thanksgiving this year with her family was fun, but I miss some of celebrations my family had when I was young.

When I was growing up Thanksgiving was an event more full of liturgy and tradition than many worship services, and in some ways just as faithful. We ate the same things in the same order, in the same room, telling the same jokes and stories, for decades, then generations. We never tired of them, and their repetition seemed to touch us in ways too deep for us to understand.

My grandfather would always act like he was too hungry for just his own meal and make passes at everybody else's plate. My mother would invariably eat too much and then tell one of us to call her a dirty name so she could get mad and chase the name caller around the block and work off the food. My brother would always lean back in his chair at the end of the meal and say, "I wonder what the poor folks are doing," implying that only the wealthy could possess such bounty as our Thanksgiving feast, and that we must have become rich to have had it. And during the cleanup, my uncle would always waddle through the kitchen clutching his stomach in mock pain saying, "Gobble, gobble, gobble," as though the abundance of his consumption had turned him into the bird itself.

We kids would roar with laughter each time we heard him do his turkey imitation. No matter how often he did it, year after year. We loved it, and we loved him for doing it. For there was something sacredly "family" about repeating the ritual time after time.

There is an ancient rabbinical story of a Jewish village that went through a ritual every year in order for God to hear their prayers. There are variations on the story, but in the one I know the people would go out into the forest, build a fire, lay out sacred stones, sprinkle water on the stones, say prayers, repeat liturgies, wait, and eventually God would hear them and answer their prayers. Over the years the people got old, the rabbi died, they couldn't carry the stones, they couldn't build a fire, and they didn't know what to do with the water. But they knew that something important happens to them in the forest, so they still went out in their infirmity to the sacred place. They would sit down wearily, look at each other, repeat a few ancient words, say some prayers and wait. And eventually God would be there and hear their prayers. And they smiled and felt loved.

I think about that story often in my church work. We don't always know why we still do the things we do, but they still move us. They still help us feel the presence of the "Holy" in ways that our logical minds can't explain. There is something mysterious about ritual and tradition—whether raising the body and blood of Jesus Christ, or clucking like a turkey on Thanksgiving—that changes us and comforts us, and gives us warmth in the cold places of our hearts. I wouldn't miss it for the world.

I enjoyed our big day with my wife's family. They are fine people and I've learned some of the rituals with which they celebrate their own version of this "Eucharistic" meal. And they're good rituals, full of life, and they always bring a smile. But they weren't the liturgies from home, the ones I was raised on and the ones I passed on, and I missed that.

I called up Karla last week just before the big day. She's thirty now, and my youngest, and she lives in Washington, DC. She, too, is far from home and this year she will be sharing thanksgiving with her fiancé and his family, and all of her someday-in-laws. She'll fit right in, though, because she's good that way. She's special and they'll love her.

"I wish I could be with you," I said.

"Me too," she said. "I sometimes miss the old days."

"I do too," I said. "But it'll be fun. You'll have a wonderful time."

"I know," she said.

I thought for a moment, and then I had to say it: "But, you know, you'll probably eat so much that you'll have to have someone call you a dirty name so you can chase them around the block to work off the food."

She laughed. "Well, that's how it is," she said. "'Gobble, gobble, gobble.'"

I laughed. And she laughed. And I loved her. And God heard our prayers.

If You Lived Here

Why Does Mikey Cry?

I have this cat that cries. Actually we used to have two cats. Geraldine was the fat one who taught me so much about how to sleep and eat with dignity and who left us nobly about a year ago. The other one is Mikey, who is getting on in years herself now, and she's the one who cries. All her life she has been trim and athletic and has even been known to take on large dogs in the neighborhood and come back looking smug. Mikey is the one who has been crying of late.

I don't mean a loud mew here and there, but a full throttle, throw back your head, open throat, piercing, wailing, cry. She'll look at doors and cry, she'll look at food and cry. At night she'll cry, in bed she'll cry. Why does Mikey cry?

I asked the Vet. I said, "What makes Mikey cry so?" But she didn't know. "Cats don't really cry," she said, but she knows animals by their bodies and not their hearts and doesn't know that Mikey cries.

Mikey has always been the tough one of the two. Long before I met either cat, more than thirteen years ago now, Mikey was a demon. The family had her front claws taken out because she terrorized the neighborhood and made curtains look like strips of pasta. But even without her claws she was hard to keep up with. I've seen Mikey climb trees with a single bound, until she was far out of reach. Geraldine, on the other hand, always viewed trees as one of nature's encumbrances, something to be walked around on her way to a sunbeam in the back yard for a nap.

For most of her life, for the better part of fifteen years, Mikey has been the strong one. She's been stoic, she's been grim. She's the one who took no guff and needed no petting. But now Mikey is old and now she cries. She cries when she wants to go outside and we open the door and a winter blast hits her in the face and she jumps back as though we've punished her. She used to go out in the cold or rain and stare back in at us as though wondering why we bi-peds were such cowards and wouldn't go outside. But now she also stays inside. She sits and looks through the glass at the deck and the yard where she used to play and strut and command respect. But the snow on the deck now hurts her bones and makes her afraid, and now she cries.

She crawls under the covers in the bed in the guest room (you wouldn't want to sleep there now) and forms a funnel with the blanket out over the heating vent to make it blow up at her with blasts of warmth, and then she whimpers and cries and goes to sleep.

She used to leap up onto the kitchen counter like super kitty to get at her food, where we keep it separated from Geraldine's own food down on the floor. We keep her dish high and away because Geraldine would eat all of her own food, and then Mikey's and ours and half the town, if we'd chop it up for her and put it in a bowl. But it's safe up there because Geraldine never wanted anything badly enough to jump up off the ground to get it. But now Mikey looks up at the food on the counter where she used to lunge with a single bound, and now she cries.

Her body, which used to be her defense against the evils of the world, is no longer her friend. It hurts now, and moves slowly and I think its weakness frightens her. She can't understand why she's no longer strong, she only knows that something is going terribly wrong and she doesn't understand why.

My wife says that Mikey has arthritis and she hurts when she moves, and I think that's true, but the cries are also cries of fear and terror. Not just pain. She hurts, but she also doesn't know why she hurts. She's weak, but she doesn't know why she's weak, so the cries come more from soul and heart than joints and bones.

She doesn't see as well as she did and barely hears at all. At times she recognizes us, and all is well, but sometimes she forgets and thinks we are strangers, "bad people" coming to get her and harm her. Why aren't things still good, and easy and fun, like they used to be? That's the great question she asks, and I suppose we ask too. Why did she have good health as though she deserved it and then have it taken away and not be told why or told how she should learn to exist at all without it? It's the not understanding that makes her cry.

I've seen her at the litter box aching to get her bowels to move. They hurt and they shouldn't, and no one can tell her why. We watch her from a distance and we want to help, we want to say it will all be okay, but it won't. One of these days life won't ever be okay for Mikey again.

I think she cries in part because of hurt, but more because of fear. She cries over the mystery of fading glory, of age overpowering youth. I think her cries are outrage at how we who have always taken care of her have fallen down on our jobs. I think her cries are the cries that Bev and I and all the rest of us will eventually make, when we sense that one day our lives won't be okay again. They will be cries of pain, but also fear. They will be cries of bewilderment, and anger, and longing for understanding. I think Mikey's cries come from someplace deeper than fur or bones or bowels or eyes. I think in her own special way, her cries are prayers. I think maybe in our own way, that's what our cries are too.

If You Lived Here

Cousin Letter

September 13, 1998

President William Jefferson Clinton
The White House,
Washington, DC 20500

Dear Bill:

It's been a long time since we have spoken. My recollection is that you made it to Aunt Gladys' funeral, but not to my father's, so it has been a long time. You probably wouldn't even recognize me today because we've both aged a bit. I was a couple of years younger than you and a part of that gaggle of cousins who terrorized the family gatherings in Hope, where your family lived, and Norphlet, where my family lived. I've missed those Christmas and Thanksgiving get-togethers, and I'll bet you do too. Somehow the problems we had back then, like eating too much turkey or not getting our turn on the swing set, seem a lot less stressful than some of the problems that we, and maybe especially you, have been enduring as adults.

We didn't talk much when we were little—we couldn't, because the two-year difference in our ages put generations between us—but I wish we had.

I have two very distinct memories of you from our family gatherings in Arkansas, and for good or ill they have helped form my thoughts about you all of our adult and very separate lives.

The first was the time when about four or five of us little boys were all trying to ride on the same horse at the same time. I don't remember who suggested it or how we did it. All I remember is being terrified once I got up there. Everyone was wiggling back and forth and yelling things like "giddyup," and "Ride 'em cowboy," and I was very near to falling off. Then, just as I was certain that I was about to fly into the air and meet my maker, I heard you yell real loud, with a voice of near-adult authority, "Don't bounce!" and all of us grew real quiet. The next thing I knew some grown-up was taking us off the poor horse and I was safe.

Where did that come from Bill? Was it from some early sense and skill at leadership, or just because you were as scared as I was, but that you knew how to control your fear and use it to yell louder than the rest of us? I wondered about that off and on over the years, especially after you became governor and then president. What drives you Bill? What makes you take control so well? Is it fear? Or leadership?

The second memory is a quick one. It happened just before we sat down for supper on somebody's backyard. I think it was Aunt Gladys and Uncle Frank's, but I'm not sure anymore. All of us had been playing hard and were thirsty, and we were lined up at the picnic table to get our allotment of Kool-Aid for supper. I was about halfway down the line of cousins and friends and you were way at the front. We waited for what seemed like hours and then one of the adults said something like, "Oh no, now there's not any left for the others." You had stood there in line in front of that cooler and drank down three tall tumblers of Kool-Aid because you were hot and thirsty, and that meant the rest of us had to drink that terrible iced tea made for the grown-ups. I was furious. We all were, but your appetite had gotten out of hand and there was nothing we could do about it. I remember I cried and cried and finally mom punished me by not letting me have any apple pie for dessert.

I've never forgotten about that, Bill. I wondered about it every time I heard that you did something superhuman, like eat more than anyone else at a state dinner, or stay up all night long playing the saxophone at your inauguration parties. Where does that appetite come from? Does it control you, or do you control it? I've never been sure.

And I've also never forgiven you for it either. And that's why I'm writing you now. I've done a lot of thinking about forgiveness in the last few days, and I felt like I ought to talk to you about it. I should have forgiven you back then, I think. Forgiveness gets easier when you have had practice at it from an early age.

Should we forgive you today? That's what I'm wondering now. There is a lot of talk about whether or not your recent apologies have sounded sincere. True forgiveness generally (though not always) follows a true and sincere apology. The fact that some of your apologies didn't sound all that sincere didn't bother me. They've been more than adequate considering that you are a politician. It's a wonder you apologized at all. Washington DC Mayor Marion Barry never apologized when he was filmed smoking crack cocaine with a prostitute. Senator Robert Packwood never apologized when he got caught sexually harassing over twenty women in his office.

What bothered me was not your sincerity. I truly believe that you are sincere. What bothered me is that you waited until Kenneth Starr's report was about to come out before you gave your apologies. It was like someone put a gun to your head and said Apologize or I'll shoot. I'd be very sincere under those circumstances too. Fox-hole confessions always strike me as sincere, just a little late. What would have impressed me more is if you had done it seven months earlier (or, of course, if you had never committed the sin in the first place, but that's for another letter).

The question is, Should I forgive you now? Incidentally, I've also not been impressed with the claim that everybody does it today, that half of the presidents, going all the way back to Jefferson and Washington, and most of congress—Democrats and Republicans—have had immoral, often distasteful, affairs. That may be true, but the fact that there are a lot of sinners in office does not help me with my question of whether I can forgive *you*. Let the rest of congress get their own family letters. I can only wrestle with forgiveness with one person at a time.

I've asked myself What would Jesus say to this situation? I remember a story in Matthew where Peter came up to Jesus and said, "Y'know, if someone sins against me, how many times should I forgive 'em? Is seven times enough?" He thought that was being generous. But Jesus said, "Not seven times, but seven times seventy" (Mt. 18:21-22). That verse helps, but there should be more to it than that. If every person, every time, receives blanket forgiveness for every crime, then there's not much distinction between any of us, and our sense of good and evil becomes a little vague.

There's another story about a woman who was caught in adultery and was brought to Jesus at the temple (John 8:1-12). They didn't have depositions or phone taps, but they were pretty sure she was guilty. (And by the way, the law in those days was that she should be stoned to death, so keep that in mind when you start thinking about how bad impeachment might be.) But Jesus doodled in the sand for a while and then looked up and said, "Any Congressman among you who is without sin may cast the first stone." The crowd began to thin out pretty quickly, until there was nobody left but Jesus and the woman. I wonder what it would look like if someone stood up in the impeachment hearings and said that...would there be a different tone to the speeches than we heard during the Whitewater hearings?

Along those lines I remember another story where Jesus tells about a farmer whose wheat crop got tainted with a bunch of nasty weeds. His workers said, "Should we go in there and separate the good wheat from the bad weeds?" The farmer (who stands for God in the story) said "No, that's my job. If you go in there and try to judge the good and the bad weeds you'll just make a mess of it and throw out a lot of the good with the bad" (Matthew 13:30). That lets me off the hook about judging people. It's not my job to judge, and besides I think Jesus is saying that I would probably get it all wrong if I tried.

But the other half of the story of the woman at the temple applies to you. After everybody left, Jesus looked at the woman and said, "Anyone here left to condemn you?" She said, "I don't see any." So he said, "Neither do I." He forgave her, simple as that. (Ever notice how Jesus always seems to deal more harshly with people whose sins had to do with politics or wealth and more gently with those whose sins were of the flesh?) But then he said something to her I've wanted to say to you: "Go and sin no more." That's a piece that seems to be missing from your story. Your appetites always seem more powerful than your ability to control them. At least up to now.

Remember that commitment you made back when you turned forty, to stop having sex outside of your marriage? Hillary and a whole lot of friends accepted that, and forgave you and stood by you when you tried to put your life back together again. Remember the apology you gave to Hillary and Chelsea back in 1992 when the whole sordid thing about Gennifer Flowers came out? You weren't too explicit about it, but we could tell that you had had a pretty painful conversation with them about it all, and we forgave you. A lot of people voted for you later on, in large part because of that apology. It made it possible to forgive you. We want to forgive you, but you don't make it easy.

I think the story that helps me the most is the Prodigal Son. He sinned and was forgiven, but he first had to pay a serious price. He was the guy who took all of his inheritance early and wasted it on wine, women, and song. From all indications he did some serious sinning with that money. When the money ran out, he was on the bottom. He was ruined. He'd lost everything. He was in fact very near to starvation before his fox hole conversion statements about repentance began to come to him. His father forgave him, but he had to go through hell and back before being able to turn around and authentically ask for his father's forgiveness.

So I guess I've come to the point of saying that, yes, you must be forgiven. After all it is God who actually does the real forgiving here and not the rest of us. All we can do is be the messenger of God's forgiveness. But at the same time true forgiveness—the kind in which the repentant sinner truly receives the forgiveness and is able to go and sin no more—only comes about, I think, when there is some kind of penalty, some kind of penance done by the sinner.

So what should that be? It's possible that you will resign, but that's up to you. It's also possible that you will be impeached, but I think that's unlikely. Neither the Democrats nor the Republicans are interested in running against an incumbent Al Gore in the next election.

You may be please to know that I don't think you should either resign or be impeached. But that's only because I think the world is far too dangerous right now to change leadership, and my feelings could change. There are gay people in the military whose careers were ruined by sexual affairs that were far more moral than yours, while you watched as commander in chief and did nothing. Congress needs the wisdom to punish you without at the same time punishing the nation. And congress is not known for its wisdom.

But even if you stay in office, that doesn't mean you should go unpunished. Various other punishments are being discussed, like being censured. But even if that doesn't come to pass, I believe that God is already at work on your penance. I can think of two or three appropriate punishments already happening, and more may come. These may not be legal punishments, but they are still very severe.

One of them is your place in history. Because of your repeated, awful, sinful behavior, your coveted, vaunted place in history has been shredded. From what we've heard, you really wanted to be one of the great presidents that people look up to and little kids want to grow up to be. That's a wonderful goal, but now you are going down in history as the guy who had oral sex while talking to a congressman on the phone. That's your legacy, Bill, and you created it for yourself. Kenneth Starr may be a partisan Republican, Linda Tripp may be a snitch, Newt Gingrich may be a whiner, but none of them are to blame for what you did. Your place in history is ruined and you did that to yourself.

Second, you've got a wife. I don't want to be funny about this, but your place in her home will never be the same again. She may possibly leave you when you get out of office, but worse than that, she may not. You have brought humiliation and ridicule on your household, and now you may be destined to live out the rest of your life with a person who hates you.

Third, you have a daughter, a good daughter whom you love a lot. She is going to have to live with the fact that graphic, ugly details of her father's uncontrollable sexual appetite, and his needy immoral behavior has been plastered across every major newspaper in the nation. So, part of your punishment is that for the rest of your life you are going to have to look her in the eyes. I think she will eventually forgive you. She's a good person, and you've raised her well. But if that happens, it will have to be a forgiveness based on authentic confession and authentic repentance, and you should absolutely go and sin no more. Until then, you are going to be punished mightily and severely every time she looks at you and remembers what you did. That will be an awful punishment.

* * * * * *

So I guess I forgive you too, Bill, though I realize that God did it first. The fact is we are all a part of God's family and God forgives us before we even ask. God created us for goodness and all of us fall from that goodness, though not all of us fall as far as you have. But when we do, the path is to confess, ask forgiveness, and then repent. That's *repent*. It means change our behavior. You're going to have to be very serious about that last one this time, Bill. You're running out of time. Your whole life depends on it. The nation depends on it. In some ways our very scary world depends on it. Don't let us down.

Well, that's it, but one last thing. I guess I have to say something nice in closing. Maybe it's because we're family, but I like to think it's also because we're all fallen human beings in need of forgiveness and all part of God's family.

One of these days, when some of the dust finally settles on all this, and eventually it probably will, give me a call. We'll have you over for a cookout on the deck and talk about old times. I'll call my brother and a couple of cousins and we'll have a family reunion just like the old days. We'll even let you talk about Social Security, welfare reform, and international debt—all those policy wonk things you love to talk about. You'll love it. However, if just once, just once, I catch you standing by the cooler and drinking down all the Kool-Aid, so that all I've got left to drink is some of that terrible old iced tea, then don't expect to get one dab of apple pie when it comes time for dessert.

In Christ's name,

(cousin) Rev. Dr. Stan Granot (Blythe) Duncan

If You Lived Here

Funny How Things Turn Out

November, 2006

I was thinking the other day about how sometimes our early experiences can influence the way we believe and behave for the rest of our lives. I have a friend, for example, whose father beat her mother, left the family when she was very young, and she never met him again until she was in her mid forties. Because of that she has always had trouble referring to God as "Father." When someone puts "God" and "Father" together she thinks of a man who beats his wife and abandons his kids. That doesn't work too well as a concept for God. She says that while her father thought he was simply proclaiming his God-given right to abandon his family, in actual fact he was helping create a social liberal and religious feminist.

You never know how God is going to use things that happen to you for purposes that you would never expect.

A few years ago I was at a national meeting of "Jubilee USA." That's the activist organization that works to cancel some of the ancient loans that are crippling the economies of poor countries around the world. It was on the weekend of Martin Luther King Sunday, and our group leader asked us to share the story of an early event that had influenced us to become involved with this and similar equality and justice campaigns. I thought and thought and then finally told the story that happened back in Oklahoma City, when African Americans were moving into our middle-class white neighborhood. When my parents heard about it they got angry and decided that we had to get out of there to protect our property values. So we moved across town to a new (and better protected) white neighborhood and I stayed there until I graduated from high school.

Now, I was just a kid when this took place and I didn't know anything about racism. But what I *did* know was that moving away from my friends felt awful. There was this cool black guy in my shop class who I liked a lot and looked up to because he was funny and he made a better wooden lamp than I did. And there was a really cute black girl in my home room class who flirted with me and made me blush and when we moved away I missed her. I always wondered what happened to both of them.

I didn't have any complicated philosophy of race and class in those days. This was long before King led busing strikes in Montgomery, was jailed in Birmingham or marched on Washington. I just missed my friends, and I was mad that my parents ripped me from my home and made me a stranger in a new school just so that we could maintain our race and property values. And here I was, still haunted by it decades later, telling it to a national meeting of activists who were wrestling with how to keep poor farmers in developing countries from being ripped from their homes and turned into strangers, immigrants, rebels, or sweat shop workers so that the US could maintain its high standard of living. I had never told the story before, but as I shared it with the others, I realized that it had had a profound impact on me for all of my life.

We went around the room with each person adding their story until finally our group leader shared hers. She was an African-American teacher, who leads these kinds of groups as a "ministry." Her story took place when she was a child in an all-white neighborhood in another state. One day she was in her front lawn playing with a large blond-haired doll that was so tall it was almost her own size. A car stopped suddenly in the street and a white man leaped out and ran up to her and jerked the doll out of her hands. He yelled at her saying "What's a N— girl like you doing playing with a white baby like that?" Then he looked in his hands and realized that he was holding a doll. It just *looked* like a white baby. He was humiliated at his mistake. He threw the doll down in the grass and stormed angrily back to his car and drove away. She started crying. It was the first time that this little girl—now an adult leading our group—had ever realized that she could be judged for her race, and the image stayed with her forever. It became one of the most powerful images of her life. It's funny how events of our childhood can drive us to opinions and vocations many years later when we are adults. That man in the car thought he was teaching a lesson to a little black girl about her rightful place in God's racial hierarchy. But instead he was helping create a thoughtful, progressive woman who spends her time teaching children and helping adults recognize and overcome their embedded racism.

She said that she had shared that story with all of her little friends up and down Everest Street, where she lived, and all of them were equally shocked by the experience.

Just then something felt strange about her story. Everest Street? I rose up out of my chair and looked at her. She began too look very familiar. "Excuse me," I said.

"Yes?" she said.

"I was just wondering," I said. "What homeroom were you in, when you were in the seventh grade?"

It's funny how things that happen to us at an early age can touch us, and change us, and form us, for the rest of our entire lives.

If You Lived Here

Never Put a Period

The story is told that years ago when comedienne Gracie Allen was ill and very close to dying, her husband, George Burns, was in such grief and sorrow that he could barely speak or function. They had been together since their 20s and had spent nearly their entire adult lives together. Burns told her that not only did he not want her to die but that he also did not want to stay here on earth without her. It would be the end of everything he loved and trusted in life.

Gracie was a devout Catholic but George was a doubting Jew. He had lost his faith in his teens when his father, who was a cantor at the synagogue, died miserably in the flu epidemic of 1903. But now, as she was succumbing to a long illness and a heart attack, Gracie, the believer, wrote a note of comfort to her theologically suspicious husband. In it she said simply, "George, never put a period where God has put a comma." He would later share those profound little words with numerous friends throughout the rest of his life. Because of that they have traveled around the world and my own church denomination has even recently adopted them as a kind of national slogan.

Notice that she didn't say, "don't worry, George, God will not let me die." She didn't say, "God will do a magic trick and make all of this right again." Those statements would have been lies. What she did say, I think, was that we should not automatically close the book, throw in the towel, and give up living when something awful happens, even if that something is the loss of a spouse or friend or even the pending loss of our own lives. When we are living in the midst of our grief, we tend to believe that life itself is broken and can never be mended. We tend to put a period at the end of those events and say that sorrow and loss are the conclusion of living itself. But most of the time they are not. God sees those events as commas, not periods. They may be hard times or tough times, but not end times.

I think of her simple words now and then when I see someone who has gone through incredible loss, yet manages to go forward in life and then experience some of the real possibilities for joy that are still in life. I think to myself that that person has really "got it."

When I was growing up in Oklahoma City, there was an "old" woman in my church (probably no more than in her mid-50s) who was involved in the Civil Rights campaign. She worked to integrate our local church, she lobbied our congressional delegation for the Civil Rights Act, and she participated in "sit-ins" and marched in demonstrations. She did more than any other white person whom I ever knew to make Oklahoma City a more equal and humane place.

But at the same time she was someone who had gone through some incredible personal pain. She had lost her husband to lung cancer and two sons to the war in Vietnam. And she also spent a great deal of her time caring for a daughter who had moved home at age 30 with some kind of congenital disease that was slowly draining her life away.

A few years ago I was back home again and someone asked me to participate in the annual "CROP Walk," which is a walk to raise money to alleviate world hunger sponsored by Church World Service.

I said sure.

We seldom have those up in New England, so I was glad to join in. Sure enough, on that bright sunny Saturday afternoon I happened to see my old friend walking along regally in the crowd. She was now looking almost ancient and she had a cane, but I still recognized her. I joined her for a while as she limped and occasionally winced, but still beamed with pride that she was able to be out there at all. It was so good to see her again and I told her so, but I knew that this had to be painful.

"Why are you even out here? What keeps you coming out for things like this?" I asked her.

I'll never forget what she said.

She first laughed, a big face-crinkling laugh. "I don't really know," she said. "But maybe when you've been through hell yourself you learn to identify and sympathize with the hell of someone else."

I don't know if George Burns ever participated in a protest march after the pain he endured from the slow death of his beloved wife. Or if he joined in a crusade to end war and racism and poverty, though I would like to think he did. What I do know is that after Gracie had died he often would tell his friends that her words, that God never gives us periods, only commas, was the one true thing that allowed him to keep his faith - or perhaps rejuvenate his faith - for all of the years after she left.

God doesn't cause the sufferings that we experience in our lives. Just being alive creates most of those. But God does give us the gift of presence and support, of companionship and care. God gives us the ability to know that bumps on the road are not walls, and that on the other side of the bumps are the possibilities of years of love, beauty and peace.

If You Lived Here

And It Was Enough

It's funny, when I was a young adult most of what I learned about faith I learned from my kids. Now that they've grown up and I've grown old, my best spiritual wisdom seems to come from my geriatric cats.

Mikey is our last remaining feline family member. She is 18 and slowly dying with a bad heart and an odd neurological disease that I never quite understood (though it's true we always accused her of being a bit "sick in the head" even when she was young and well). The doctors gave her six months to live, but that was about seven months ago. Today she continues to confound the odds and find life worth living, even when each day there is less and less of it for her to live. I think she knows she is dying and may even know that it's coming soon, but as long as it doesn't get in the way of her important tasks (sleeping, eating, cuddling), she doesn't say much about it. And when she does, it's usually more of a grudging admission than despair or defeat.

I suspect that more often than not, when someone decides to remain alive to the very end of life, it's a decision based on faith and not facts. All of us are dying, no one gets out alive, and no one has much say about the spot where our names fall on the list. But how we decide to treat our spot is determined by our faith.

That reminds me of prayer. I know on the one hand that there are authentic occasions when prayer contributed to healing, but I also know that it doesn't happen very often, and that people who count on it are often disappointed. My most authentic prayers in life were probably not when I was asking God to change the things around me but when I asked God to change me in light of them. Not to change my father after a brutal accident crushed the life out of him, but to change me in the world in light of the accident. God's love doesn't take away death, the apostle Paul once famously said, but it can take away its "sting."

I was in my office at home pondering this the other day when Mikey came in to see me. She must have been hurting more than usual that day because she stood anxiously in the doorway crying wildly for me to turn and help her. Something was terribly wrong, she said, and she was sure it was the awful food in her bowl. I got up and changed it and moments later she was back. No, it was because the water is too cold, so I changed that. Then it was that the litter box was too dirty, or her bed was too lumpy, or the weather was too rainy, or the house was too chilly. Each item I worked on dutifully until finally I saw that could no longer help her. I had run out of fixes for the things around the house that she blamed for the misery of her life.

"Mikey," I said to her, "You're just sick. I can't fix that." But she still cried. "There's just nothing I can ultimately do to change the things that are going wrong in you. I want to help, but I can't." She cried like I was somehow the higher power that could transform the disease that was eating at her, the ache that she couldn't understand, and that I wasn't fulfilling my responsibilities. "I'm sorry, Mikey," I said. "I'm very, very sorry."

I reached down then and picked her up again and just held her for a moment in my arms. I've got to say she looked awful. She used to be young and vibrant and her fur felt like silky magic when you rubbed it. It would glow when you stroked it. But today it's mottled and patchy and she's lost too much weight. I've always hated cats, and I never thought I'd say this, but that night I held her and looked at her and could still see the young healthy kitty that I had first met more than a decade earlier, and I told her she still looked beautiful. Time makes people blind. It's a gift of God.

"Mikey," I said to her. "I can't offer much. I don't have much. All I've got are arms and hugs and love from a wounded old human for a dying old cat. I can't make the pain go away, but I can help you know that you are still loved in the midst of it, and maybe that's enough."

I cradled her in my arms and carried her through the house, petting her and showing her all of her favorite spots and foods and chairs that have brought her warmth and pleasure through the years. By the time we returned to my office she had grown more calm. She was purring. I laid her down and then she fell asleep. She had prayed for youth or healing or relief from pains of the end time that terrified her, and in actual fact all I could give her was a tour of the house. But in actual fact it was enough. Sometimes the answers to our prayers change nothing in the physical world, but they change our sense of being loved in our interior world, and it is enough.

If You Lived Here

Benny's Body

My step-father was a musician. A piano player, to be specific. He's probably where I got my interest in the piano. "Back in the day," he used to move around a lot with the likes of big bands like Tommy Dorsey's and other lesser-knowns before he settled down and married a wife with two very non-movable kids. Even though he never actually "taught" me the piano, I think I picked up a lot of tidbits about music from him by osmosis, because he was in our family during most of my adolescent (impressionable) years. He had stories of his adventures in the business that I've never forgotten. Like the time he played the calliope in the circus just over the lion's cage and the lions would lick at his feet as he hit the peddles. He started chewing tobacco so he could spit at the lions to discourage them from licking his feet. He finally got fired from the job because one of the lions was going blind in one eye and the owner suspected that my step-dad's tobacco was the cause. Or the time he played one of those portable organs on wheels in the back of a pickup in a Shriners' parade. The pickup slowed down too long one time and then had to take off so fast that his platform with the organ and his bench burst out the back end of the pickup and rolled down the hill. The crowds went wild. They thought it was part of the show. He was a good showman and tried to keep on playing, acting like nothing was wrong, but eventually he slammed into a hot dog stand and pickles, mustard, and Stanley Steamers went everywhere. It must have been a glorious sight.

One day he played the organ at a funeral for Benny Moran, one of his musician buddies who was married to a huge woman named Inez, from the Genoese family. You may recall that two of the brothers in "The Godfather" were based on real-life brothers in the Genoese family. My step father said they asked him to play a medley of Frank Sinatra songs at the end of the funeral while the family and friends processed by the casket for the final viewing of Benny's body. At the end of the procession, as they brought Inez up to the casket, he launched into "I'll Do it My Way," and Inez burst into tears. "That was our song!" she wailed. She began screaming and swooning and beating on the casket, and then beating on Benny. "Why did you die?" she cried. "God, I loved you so." Some of her brothers jumped up to try and hold her back, but she was bigger than they were and they couldn't stop her. "We sang that song together," she screamed, beating on Benny's chest and pulling and tugging on the casket. Finally, she evidently lost her balance and fell backward and pulled the casket, the lid, and most of Benny's body right down on top of her onto the floor.

The crowd was aghast. The funeral parlor folks and the brothers swarmed around her to get her on her feet again and to stuff Benny back where he came from and try to recapture the decorum of the occasion. But while they were wrestling with him someone noticed a bank bag was tucked between Benny's legs and they pulled on it. It had just under a million dollars in it.

It turns out that a couple of months earlier, when Benny's health was beginning to fail, one of his many brothers-in-law, who had embezzled this money from the family's illegal gambling enterprises, had bribed the funeral parlor owner to hide it until Benny died and then stuff it between Benny's legs and bury it in the cemetery with him. As I recall, he was planning on leaving it there for a while, and then retiring to the Bahamas after people had stopped looking around for it.

However, the family got wind of the embezzlement thing and the day before the funeral the brother-in-law skipped the country without taking his money with him. The funeral parlor director didn't know about any of this, so he went ahead as planned and stuffed the money in between Benny's legs just like he promised. On the other hand, since the money fell out at such a public gathering as a funeral, no one in the family wanted to admit that the unfortunate filthy lucre was actually theirs. The funeral parlor guy couldn't say anything about it because it would be admitting that he'd been bribed to put it there. The police who investigated couldn't say anything because some of them had been in on some of the unseemly tasks of acquiring it in the first place. When the remaining brothers regained their composure, they got together in the back of the funeral parlor for a moment and then announced to the gathering that this money must be Benny's long lost family savings and how happy they all were—in spite of the looks on their faces—that Inez had finally found it. Inez didn't know anything about any long-lost savings, but she also didn't want to say anything because here she was at her husband's funeral being handed a half a million dollars just for beating on her husband's chest, something she'd been doing without charge for years while he was alive.

They all decided that a lot of publicity about the event wouldn't be prudent. They declared it to be a good day, a good funeral and all went out to Colonel Sanders for the collation. My dad got a thousand bucks for his services (in cash, unmarked bills, as I recall) because he'd played those Sinatra songs so sweetly. Inez retired to Las Vegas and last we heard she was part owner of a casino. My mother tells me that not too long ago she read in the paper that a fellow named Genoese, who lived in the Bahamas, was arrested over in the local cemetery trying to dig up the body of his dearly departed, deceased brother-in-law, Benny. The article said no one knew why he was doing it. Probably just remorse, they said. Probably he just wanted to see the body one last time.

If You Lived Here

The Relations We Have

September, 2004

My mother finally died this past summer. It was early in the morning on the fourth of July, and it was painless, in her sleep. She lived in Oklahoma, and had been sliding into death for some time. Last December I had made a nostalgic trip out there to help shut down her home and move her into assisted living. So while her final passing wasn't unexpected, I had hoped that she might have at least a few more years in her new surroundings.

In fact, we had talked just days before she died about the possibility of my getting to Minneapolis where my son lives. I could take pictures of my new grand baby, I told her, and come show them to her. She loved the idea and laughed a rare laugh about it.

I will miss that laugh and I will miss her. She was a dear who didn't deserve the kind of life she suffered for the past several years. In little more than a decade, she had lost her businesses, her husband, her sight, her home, and finally her health. There is, perhaps, no such thing as a "good" death, but in many cases there is at least a "sigh of relief" death, and this was one of them.

Ironically, just as we received the news about my mother, my wife and I were packing to go to Maine, to hold a memorial service and scatter the ashes of her mother who had passed away just a few weeks earlier. I had to leave my wife's emotional family gathering early to fly home for one of my own.

Back at home the next day, waiting for my plane to Oklahoma, I picked up my messages and found out that I needed to call my congressman about an upcoming Congressional vote on Third World debt cancellation. There were stewardship and counseling center meetings coming up, and several dear people in the congregation were ill and needed a visit from me.

Reading the messages, though, all I could really feel was fatigue. I didn't have the energy to call anybody. Even a pastor gets tired on occasion. When I was younger I was either bullet proof or dishonest, but I seemed better able to handle these things.

As I've aged I've become a bleeder, and today the pain of others too easily becomes my own. It's a casualty of love, I think. Maybe longevity. Maybe both.

When I got to Oklahoma we had a lovely service out at the cemetery. It was very simple and only family and friends came. The minister said prayers and read scripture and we all wept.

Mom's dearest friend in the world was there. He owns a party store and brought balloons for each of us, which we held during the service. We tied one to the casket that held her "earthly tent," and looked at it somberly during the readings.

At one point my mother's balloon got loose from the casket and shot out from under the canopy, straight off into the distance, still visible for several minutes.

"My God," said my cousin sitting next to me. "It's your Mom. It's her spirit going off, saying goodbye."

After the service and the meal that followed, I took some time to drive by and see some friends I've known and loved for many lifetimes but too often taken for granted.

They're down there and I'm up here, and I've just assumed that they would always be around. But one day they won't be, and this may have been the last time I could just drive by and say hello. We hugged and cried and shared old stories.

There was something mysteriously redemptive about the visit. It's very healing to be hugged by someone who loves you for just having shown up. It's a gift of God, the grace of God.

In a world that is going increasingly crazy, friends and family are the connecting links to the Holy Spirit. The older I get, the more I realize that the relationships we have are the relationships we have. They're hard to create but easy to squander.

Life is precious. It's on loan from God for only a short amount of time and you never know when you're due to give it back.

Maybe learning to bleed is the first step toward appreciating life and learning to love. And maybe there are worse things to happen to us than becoming casualties of love.

If You Lived Here

The Meaning of Aceh

January, 2005

Years ago in my little town of Heavener, Okla., (population 1,800), an old man got gangrene in his leg and had to have it amputated. It was an awful thing. He had diabetes and after years of treatment the only thing the doctors knew to do was to cut out the dying parts of his body to save the rest.

One night not long after that, at a reception following our town-wide Thanksgiving service, a well-intentioned preacher in the community commented that it was surely the man's sin that caused it to happen.

"I knew him when we was boys," he said to us across the snack table. "He had too many women that weren't his wife, and now God's taken that leg off him to teach him the wages of sin."

That didn't sound quite right, but I was younger than he was, so what did I know? Then from somewhere in back of me, Charlie Wilson, a Methodist and a recovering alcoholic, who knew a thing or two about sin himself, yelled, "If God was in the business of ripping off legs when somebody messed around some when they was young, then every man, woman and child in this town over the age of 15 would be walking around today with a limp."

Today that reminds me of a cruel theology, popular among many of us Christians, that says that when a person dies or gets hurt it is because God did it, to teach us or test us or punish us our sins.

But that belief is wrong. And believing it sets us up for a terrible unbelief when we hear of an innocent father in Banda Aceh having his equally innocent baby torn from his arms by the uncontrollable waters of one of the worst tsunamis in history. It is a theology that works fine when you are talking about God punishing Adolf Hitler or Saddam Hussein, but it fails badly when you're talking about tidal waves and dying babies.

When I was young, my parents divorced. Eventually my father met another woman who was visiting family in Heavener and they got engaged. But then one evening—one week before their marriage—they were returning home from a party when two teen boys in a pickup, who had been drinking beer in a corn field, drove straight into them on their way back to town for more beer. They all were killed instantly. But God did not do that.

After my parents divorced my mother married again to a nice man with silver hair and a Maine accent who loved her deeply, but who had a series of long and ugly strokes that ground him down and drained his life for five eternal years until finally he begged her to let him die to get relief from the horror of meaningless living. And God didn't do that either.

God doesn't kill people. Storms, tsunamis, earthquakes, and human sins kill people. God didn't cause the nightmares of Indonesia and Southeast Asia any more than God caused the mudslides in California or the idolatrous ideologies that drove us to war in Iraq. It is true that God is very much in the storms and wars, but God is in the healing not the killing. God is in the mending not the destroying.

God lives and moves in the midst of suffering, but as its resolution, not its cause. God is in the relief workers, the doctors, the volunteers, the soldiers, the helicopters, and in the heroic acts of countless nameless people who risked their lives, saved their neighbors and rescued survivors.

God's fundamental act in the universe is salvation, making the creation one, more whole, more "good," and when the creation invariably fails or falls, God is in the midst of the hurt working for some kind of reconciliation in the brokenness.

Maybe when we ask, what is the meaning of the tragedy itself, we miss the point. Maybe meaning is actually what we give to an event in its aftermath. We make meaning from meaninglessness when we place our hands in God's hands and stick them into the healing. It is how we respond to an event that gives it meaning.

When Charlie made his uppity comment about God giving us all a limp to punish us for our sins, the preacher turned away in a huff, and I don't think they ever spoke again. I don't think he ever forgave Charlie for his radical theology. And I don't think I ever appropriately thanked him.

If You Lived Here

When is it Time?

November, 2001

Mikey's crying has gotten worse. The vet doesn't know exactly why. Maybe it's her heart because it's old and it races too fast for her aging body. Maybe it's her failing kidneys and damaged bowels that are old and diseased and hurt her in ways she could never understand. Maybe it's feline Alzheimer's that confuses her and weakens her and frightens her. Maybe it's just that she misses Geraldine, her companion for life, who died six months ago, just about the time that Mikey's crying started getting worse. When she was younger she could role with changes like that, but now she's old and maybe major losses throw her off and she can't recover well. Maybe she's just old.

She cries now at more random times and in more awful ways. She has a rhythmic, rolling scream that starts low and then builds, louder and louder until the house is filled with her pain. She sometimes doesn't recognize us, or her surroundings, or her bed. At night she is so loud that we have had to restrain her so that we can sleep. We lock her in the laundry room and then turn on a fan for "white noise." There, she rages at whatever monsters live in her stomach, or ghosts in her mind, and we can get a few hours of rest.

The vet has given her heart medicine, and sleep inducing medicine, and liver medicine, but so far the only things that seem to work are hugs. In the midst of her wails, we sometimes just take her and hold her and that sometimes calms her. She sometimes knows us, and sometimes doesn't. But I think she does know that out there, someone bigger is loving her and holding her, and it drives demons away for a time.

The vet gave her six months at this pace, and so far she's lasted three. We don't really know what to do. We've talked about it, and about Mikey's future, and we don't know what would be the best thing, the most "humane" thing. When we talk over Mikey's options, we aren't discussing a pet with food bowls and litter boxes and shedding fur, but a dear aging woman who helped raise the kids, when they were teens, comforted us when we were lonely, kept our lives organized in terms of meals, potty breaks and nap times.

"When should we do it?" My wife asked one night at dinner, when Mikey's agony was particularly horrible. "When should we decide that she can't go on like this any longer?"

I don't like questions like that. Who wants to have the power to decide when a family member lives or dies? But we have to make some kind of decision eventually, and we don't know when or how to make it. There is a time, though I don't know exactly when it is, when life just doesn't have enough fun in it any more, when the balance finally goes the wrong way, when the joys of the goodness of living are overwhelmed the the wrenching pain of dying. But it's hard to know when that is.

"I don't think she's there yet," I said. "I think she still enjoys our company, and her little bed and her new food." We had stopped giving her dry food a few weeks earlier because it hurt her stomach and her new soft food goes down easier.

"That's not much of a life," she said. "Are we helping her or protecting us?"

What is the moral thing to do, the "Christian" thing? When you love someone, is it moral to let them suffer? Or is it moral to take the life of a loved one, who God has created and given life—never mind whether the loved one has four legs or two?

How does one evaluate and measure when an end time has finally come? How does one decide what to do when that time has come? How does one decide *what kind* of end it should be, assuming we've decided that there should be one? And who should decide?

Ironically, while we were pondering what to do with Mikey's life, the news carried the story of the US Attorney General taking the state of Oregon to court to overturn their "Death with Dignity Act," arguing that life is too precious to be terminated, no matter how awful that life may become. In their case they were debating *human* life, but the parallels were not lost on our family. When you are faced with the frightening decision of whether or when to take the life of someone you love, the number of legs of the loved one seem irrelevant.

After dinner, Mikey began to cry again. She wailed on in some combination of pain and fear. She was sitting in the hall screaming, perhaps she got lost and didn't know where she was and was scared. For a moment, we only listened, no one could talk. I finally got up and went to her, picking her up, cradling her in my arms. Mikey cried, and I hugged. Eventually the demons, whoever they were or whatever they were, went away. I held and rocked her, and the magic of grace and love worked, and she was finally calmed.

"I don't think it's time yet," I said to my wife, while I stood there holding Mikey. "I think there are still a few parts of Mikey's life that are good, very good."

"I know," she said quietly, and watching us.

And Mikey purred.

If You Lived Here

Obdulio's Roses

Spring, 1991

In the Fall of 1989 a horrible thing happened in El Salvador. A civil war was raging. The rebels had mounted a furious offensive against the nation's capital. The military-led government —considered one of the most brutal in the hemisphere—was in danger of falling. One night in the midst of the fighting, President Frederico Cristiani was roused out of bed with a message from Colonel Emilio Ponce. We have to do something dramatic to send a message, he was told. The people of the city are rising up against us. Poor people are barricading their streets, and our troops can't get through. The military was requesting authorization to commit a heinous act of massacring all of the Jesuit priests who were professors at the University of Central America in San Salvador, El Salvador. They were the target because they all had been highly visible in the campaign for a negotiated settlement of the war, and for their work in human rights. By all accounts, though he later denied it, Cristiani said yes.

On November 12, 1989, at about two o'clock in the morning, a battalion of elite, U.S.-trained, army troops broke into the university, and murdered eight people. Six were priests, one was their cook, and the other was her daughter. Two priests escaped the massacre because they were out of the country on speaking engagements. The killers left evidence everywhere, they were seen by witnesses, and they later gave confessions, yet when the case finally closed, only a handful of people were charged, fewer went to trial, and fewer still were convicted. No one did time for the killings, and none of the commanders, including Ponce or Cristiani, who gave the orders, were even indicted.

From the U.S. Congressional investigation that followed, we now know that the troops had been in a human rights training session with U.S. advisors when they were called away to do the murders, and that our advisors knew the general outline of the plans for the killings at least a week in advance of the killings. We also know that both the Salvadoran Government and the U.S. embassy have attempted to limit, or at least slow down, the investigation. But nothing came of the investigations, and now most people both here and in El Salvador have forgotten.

Public outrage at the time centered for the most part on the six priests who died that night because they were well known. However, there were other people caught in the politics of the story, and they are also significant.

One of those is Obdulio Ramos, a poor farmer, husband, and father, whose name almost nobody knows. In the late 1960s Obdulio as a young man worked on a coffee plantation in Santa Tecla, near San Salvador, the capital city of El Salvador, and the site of the later murders. At the same time that he was working on the plantation, a young woman named Elba was also living and working inside San Salvador as a domestic servant. One year, because her income was so meager, she asked her employer if she could take some time off during the upcoming coffee season and go to Santa Tecla and help work the harvest.

He agreed, and when Elba arrived at the plantation, it happened that she was assigned to the same section which was being overseen by Obdulio Ramos. They worked for several weeks together in the fields, and soon it became clear that they had fallen in love. The following year they were married and afterward she moved into his small house in Santa Tecla to begin creating a home and a family. Their life together was never easy, even in the early years when they were young and Obdulio was strong. They were always very poor and were often forced to move while looking for work or fleeing from the violence which was growing throughout El Salvador.

In 1970 Elba gave birth to their first child, a girl. Then in 1976, they had their second, a boy. In the beginning Elba tried not to work outside the home so that she could take care of their children. But by the mid-1980s, when El Salvador was experiencing what the U.S. government at the time described as a "booming" economy, the country's poverty grew so severe that she had to take a job working as cook and housekeeper for a newly established Jesuit theological center in San Salvador.

Then in 1989, a position at the University came open for a guard and groundskeeper. Fr. Amando López, one of the Jesuits who knew Obdulio through Elba's work at the center, recommended him for the position. In early August of that year they moved their family into the University's guard house, which sits at the main gate of the University and which opens up into the courtyard where the Jesuit dormitories are located.

By early fall, the family had settled into their new lives and were dreaming of a future which could finally be secure and stable. In the beginning, Obdulio spoke occasionally of wanting to grow roses in the courtyard. Roses, he said, were flowers which manage to produce beauty while surrounded by thorns. But his growing responsibilities around the University prevented him from doing any special work with flowers until late November.

Elba at the same time had gained a reputation for being an excellent cook and she won praises for her wonderful cakes and pastries. She delighted her friends and students at the university by teaching them the art of cake baking. Their daughter Celina was growing up and had just started high school. She was a catechist in the church and was secretly hoping to be married soon. The young man in question had been her boyfriend since they were fourteen, and he was planning on breaking the news to Celina's parents during Advent in December.

Elba once commented that, though she was poor and could not do much to serve her Lord, through her cooking and cleaning skills she gave the Priests the gift of free time so that their skills could be used in the peace talks and national movements for Salvadoran reconciliation. In that way, she said, she knew that she was serving God. "Of course everything is messed up here," she once said about El Salvador. "But we will never give up. With God's help we cannot give up."

The month of November, 1989, however, changed all of their plans forever. The rebels launched their assault on San Salvador, and Obdulio and Elba found their city ablaze with violence on all sides. We now know, through testimony from Salvadoran military leaders, that the country was very close to falling into rebel hands. Whole neighborhoods in the capital had risen up in support of the rebels. They tore up street stones and used them to build walls to keep the government troops out. In response, the government began bombing raids on those neighborhoods and over the weeks hundreds of civilians were killed.

On the morning of November 16, Elba went up to the theological center to do her daily work. This day, however, she took a change of clothing with her in just case the fighting became be so dangerous that she could not make her way back home that night. She did go back though. She told Fr. López that because it was so dangerous she feared for Obdulio's safety, and wanted to get back to see him again. So at the end of the day she made her way slowly through the growing darkness and sounds of gun fire back down to the guard house. She cooked dinner for Obdulio that night— the last she would ever cook for him. Then the two of them decided that it would be best if she and Celina would go back up the hill to stay in the Jesuits' dorms. They thought that with the intense fighting, it would be best if mother and daughter stayed up at the University. Their little boy was out of town visiting relatives and was safe. Obdulio had no choice but to stay at the guard house. But at least Celina and Elba, they thought, would be safe in one of the dorms at the University. No matter what happened, they thought, neither the rebels nor the government would ever do anything so heinous as to attack a seminary and kill priests. So Elba and Celina gathered up a few things for their stay and left. Obdulio kissed them goodbye and told them that he would check in on them early the next morning.

* * * * * *

No one slept well that night. There were gun shots and loud voices until far into the morning. The sky lit up with gunfire and explosions from the bombings. People in dark clothing ran through the streets firing weapons. Finally, at dawn the city-wide curfew was lifted and Obdulio hurried as fast as he could up the hill to the courtyard. There on the carefully manicured lawn he saw the bodies of five priests, mangled and bloody, lying in the grass. One was at the gate, where he had been shot letting the killers in. The sixth was missing because he had been killed in his room and never made it to the lawn. But there were two other people who were also missing, and not on the lawn. Ahead of him he saw the gate to the dormitory gardens and beyond that was the Oscar Romero Pastoral Center. The Center was still burning from the destruction of the night before, and the gate was still open. It was where the killers had come in. He hurried down the stairs toward the gate pausing to look into each of the rooms as he went until he came to the one which was most important to him. There, in the last one, inside a doorway which had been broken and burned, he saw them, Celina and Elba. They had been dead since early morning, but they were still holding one another tightly in each others' arms.

According to later confessions by the killers (which according to Salvadoran law, cannot be used against them), the two women were among the first discovered and first shot as the troops entered the University grounds. One of the priests, Ignacio Martín Baro, was not far from the dorms when he heard the shots and he ran to Elba and Celina's room. "This is an outrage," he cried when he saw what had happened. "You are scum!" He started to run into the room but one of the soldiers turned without speaking and fired at him until he fell silent onto the ground.

The killers then searched the rest of the buildings and one after the other, the priests were found and forced out onto the open lawn and shot. Altogether the soldiers were on the campus only about thirty minutes. They had been trained well for the task. They burned the university offices, stole what money they could find, and fired thousands of rounds of ammunition into the air to give the appearance of a fire-fight with the rebels.

When they had finished their work and were leaving, one of them, Sub-Sgt. Antonio Avalos, known as "Satan" by his friends, heard noises coming from the room where Elba and Celina had been. In his testimony later, he said that he shined a light into their room and saw them crying and bleeding, but still alive, holding onto one another for comfort. "Satan" had an AK-47 assault rifle which had been given to him by his commander because it looked like those used by the rebels, and it might therefore help shift blame for the killings to the rebels. He said that he pointed the rifle into the women's room and began firing again and again and again—to "re-kill" them, he said—until they finally became silent.

Days later there were funerals for all who were killed in the massacre. At the funeral for Elba and Celina, mourners were told wonderful stories of Elba's ministry of cooking, and how she taught others to bake her magnificent cakes. As the mourners came forth at the end of the mass to celebrate the Eucharist, they were surprised to see that the "body of Christ" being "broken" for them in the act of communion was none other than a big delicious Elba-style chocolate cake! Her friends, who had received her gift in life, were now celebrating that same gift in her death.

* * * * * *

I visited the University not long after the tragedy, my first visit since I had lived there as an economic researcher during the eighties. In fact, I moved back to the states less than a month before the siege, the bombings, and the massacres had taken place. I was returning this time because I was leading a seminar group studying Liberation Theology in Central America. When we arrived and got out of our bus, we walked solemnly and almost worshipfully through the gate and into the garden, past the door to the dorm room where Elba and Celina had stayed for "safety," and up the steps to the lawn where Obdulio had found the bodies of the priests, most of whom I had known during my years in the city. I stood there for a few moments imagining what it had looked like the day of the killings. It all looked so clean and harmless now. At the edge of the campus, at the foot of a steep hill, was the home where Obdulio and Elba and their young family had lived. I didn't know anything about him now. I stood there looking down for some time, and finally another delegate in our group walked up behind me. "Did you see his roses?" he said.

"See what?" I asked.

"Roses."

I looked around. I'd been lost in thought and blind to my surroundings. "No," I said. "Where are they?"

"Over there." He pointed back to the lush green lawn which had once been strewn with bodies. "He planted a rose bush there for each person who had died."

Then I saw them. They were magnificent. Two rows of vibrant red rose bushes. In the center were two that were yellow. Obdulio had finally been able to plant his roses. I pointed to the two in the middle. "Why are those different?" I asked. "They're yellow and the others are red."

"I don't know," he said.

Just then from the shadows of the trees, a man appeared to us whom we had not seen before. He had been listening to us but hadn't until now spoken. He was small, with a round face, and enormously pleasant eyes. "They are for Elba and Celina," he said quietly in Spanish.

We were unable to speak. The person who we were talking about and wanting to see had been there all along and suddenly we were mute. Neither of us could speak.

The group was beginning to call to us. Our time was up and they were leaving. We had to join them, but we didn't want to leave yet. We made some brief small talk, the other delegate hurriedly asked for a quick photo, but then we had to leave.

As we began to turn away, I looked back at Obdulio and blurted out a question. "The roses," I asked, "Why are they yellow?"

The group was yelling at me. They'd leave without me they said. "Why are they yellow"?

"I wanted them to be different from the rest," he said, smiling broadly. "I wanted people to remember my family."

Maybe this will help that happen.

If You Lived Here

And Then There Was None

April, 2001

L ast week our little cat, Mikey, died. On Maundy Thursday, almost one year to the day from when Geraldine died. While the deacons of the church were setting up the sanctuary for a service which would commemorate the initiation of Jesus from this life into the next, we were at the vet with Mikey. There, a nice woman with kind eyes and a white coat, put a syringe into Mikey's front paw and slowly took her life away.

I wouldn't mention it now, except that I have spent so much time making fun of our cats, and using them as props for other issues, that it seemed only fitting to finally finish their story. Over the years they have allowed me to say any number of things that would have been too delicate or controversial if I had just come out and said them. But nobody takes offense at a story about a cat. I've sent their stories to our local newspaper, and after a while they both began to receive their own fan mail. A woman in Quincy wrote me once saying that she took a story about Mikey to her Bible study and the whole group read it and cried. A man in Brighten said that reading about Mikey not only gave him a whole new appreciation of cats (which he previously had not had), but it also taught him something about the meaning of prayer. (That was the point.)

Even though it's true that most of the time I simply used them as foils for some larger truth, it is also true that their lives did actually teach me a lot. I believe that the lives of everyone we love should do that, human or animal, or else we've squandered a measure of the value of the relationship. Their stoicism and resiliency in the face of adversity, their ability to find (or create) humor in the midst of pain or sorrow, and (especially in Geraldine's case) their knack for knowing how to rest and take naps when life becomes stressful.

But today I realize that another important thing they taught me was not just how to live, but also how to die.

Geraldine had a tumor in her belly, and probably felt the worst when she died. But she was stoic and peaceful and survived to the end with a great sense of what was probably courage. As long as life was kept well ordered with patterns and habits that she could trust, with food and water and love from the big people, she could and did bear up for a long time and do well. When she was finally going down, we could tell, we could see it. It became clear that she was beginning to suffer so she was the first to take the trip to the vet to see the nice woman with the kind eyes and white coat, and be "put to sleep" (though I hate that phrase).

Mikey was more complicated. Her disease was in her head and it scrambled her sensibilities and jumbled her thinking. She wasn't fighting pain so much as she was fighting ghosts. She was railing against demons that only she could see, that would attack in the night and drive some of the life out of her. She would go into a room and get lost and cry because she couldn't find her way back out again. One night during her last and hardest week, she was crying terribly so I got up to help her but when she saw me she ran away like I was one of the monsters who had broken in to hurt her.

We had ongoing conversations about when and how would we know that it was Mikey's time to take her in to see the woman with the coat. It's an awful conversation to have, whether it is about a feline or family. How does one know when a life's joys and loves are finally outweighed by fears and pains? Especially when the loved one is an animal who can't speak.

But finally we knew. Mikey knew. Her behavior told us and we took her in.

One great mystery we learned from Mikey, which is not a prop or a foil, is this: there is a tremendous difference between a sickness that can be addressed by medicines, and an illness that can only be helped by hugs. Mikey's "meds" could help the pain in her head just so long and after that she had to rely on hugs. The only reason Mikey was able to live as long as she did was that she trusted that there was healing and transcendent behind those hugs. She knew what they meant and where to go to get them, and how they helped to heal her soul when she got them. The demons of the head or the body are not nearly as scary when we can realize that we are loved.

I have had all manner of friends and family die over the years, and certainly losing cats is no greater loss than some of those. I've lost family members through long grueling debilitating diseases and through sudden and brutal accidents. Some died when they were old and some when they were shockingly young. One thing I've known for a long time is that there is no good day to die. There is no "appropriate" time or way of losing someone who you love that is not at some level wrenching and painful. But it is also true that the best way to help someone you love survive with abundancy to that end of their life is by hugs. The drugs and the operations will keep their bodies alive a little while longer, the operations will mend a portion of their bones or their organs, but the soul survives through love. Don't let them down. They deserve it. You deserve it. And remind them that on the other side of the loss is new strength and new life.

If You Lived Here

My Mother's Friends

August, 2003

A Couple of years ago, I had to take an emergency flight back home to Oklahoma for the unexpected death and then funeral of my mother. She had grown old and frail and blind, and finally one day she gave up and gave in and moved on to her heavenly home with God.

While I was there I took some time to walk up and down the street where she lived to tell her neighbors what had happened and to say goodbye for the last time. Many I had known since childhood and they still lived in the old neighborhood. Across the street lived two old gay men whom I never knew well, but always appreciated because my mother told me how kind they had been to her when she had been in an accident and was no longer able to drive. When she eventually became blind they took over mowing her lawn, cleaning her gutters, and raking her leaves. One time when a truck pulled up and people started mysteriously hauling things out of her garage, they ran over to prevent what they thought was theft of their friend's household property. As it happened, the truck was from her church, and the goods were for a rummage sale, but she never forgot their attempt to rescue what she called "the old 'widder' in distress."

I knocked on their door, but no one answered so I moved on to the next house where I saw the father of a young girl I had known as a teen. I asked him what had happened to the guys next door and he said "well that's an interesting story." Evidently over the years new families had moved into the neighborhood who didn't know the two men and who were not like the older crowd, and they were upset that the neighborhood had allowed "queers" to live so close by. Young parents, inspired by teachings of a variety of new churches and television evangelists, were worried that these old men might be a danger to their children. So they began talking around the neighborhood and snubbing them, and finally the two felt the pressure and moved away. I asked the neighbor if they had ever actually done anything wrong and he said no. Actually, he said, "they was pretty good fellas." But "they were queer and all, and they say that's bad, so I guess it is."

All of this came back to me this week when a year later on July fourth, Independence Day, I happened to be in Atlanta Georgia, watching a thousand members of my church, the United Church of Christ, vote to affirm "equal marriage rights for all people, regardless of gender." That means, as most of us would have put it, "same sex marriage."

According to the way our church is governed, votes such as this are not binding on local congregations. We say that the national General Synod "speaks *to* the churches, not *for* the churches." On the other hand, it was a pretty inclusive crowd, and probably closely represents the opinions of the majority of our members nationwide. I looked around the room while they were debating the issue and saw a huge range of faces. Young people, old people, gay and straight, "red and yellow, black and white" (as the old hymn puts it), from across the U.S. and a smattering of nations. They wrestled with the issue for two days, first in committee and then on the floor, with debate, amendments, re-phrasings, and then prayer. They were attempting to discern how God might be still speaking to us in an increasingly complex and polarized world. And what the vast majority finally concluded was that no matter what one could say about the *differentness* of same gender marriage, they couldn't quite be convinced of the *wrongness* of it. How could God create human beings out of love and then tell them not to love one another?

I confess that I agree with that. At one level I didn't have a horse in that race. I'm happily and heterosexually married and I wasn't even a delegate to the Synod. But on the other hand I kept thinking of those two nice guys who looked out for my mother. The Bible says very little about homosexuality and some of the references are frankly unclear. Jesus is totally silent on it. What he is not silent on, though, is the need to love, accept, and care for all people. Bring in the poor, the hungry, the outcast, the sick, the beggars, the alienated, lonely and marginalized, he would say. He condemns wealth and war and divorce and oppression, but never two old men who love each other and mow the lawns for neighboring widows.

In one of the very few times he mentions marriage at all, he says don't get a divorce. And if we religious people really took the Bible literally, Jesus' words on divorce would cut out forty-five percent of our clergy, fifty percent of our members, and sixty-percent of Congress. I think there is a huge number of people sitting in pews today who are more than happy that God is still speaking to us today and imparting new truths to help us adapt to a new world.

When I left the assembly hall that day, I was frankly nervous. I would have to go back to my church and explain this extremely difficult decision to the good people in my congregation who had not been there and who might only know of it through headlines and sound bites. The delegates took a leap of faith that day, hoping and praying that their actions were discerning the will of a still-speaking God. But in the long run, we're all mortal and nobody knows. We all act in faith and pray that we will be forgiven if we fail.

But I was encouraged by the words of a pastor friend of mine from Texas, who told me that when he dies and stands before St. Peter at the pearly gates, and hears a list of his lifetime's sins and mistakes, he expects to hear a long, long list. But when all is said and done, he said he would much rather be judged for being too open minded than too closed. "If I'm going to make a mistake," he said, "I suspect God would rather it be a mistake of letting too many people into the kingdom than too few."

And you know, I think I agree with that too.

If You Lived Here

How Did You Sleep?

August, 2000

There is something dark and almost evil about the way that we in the U.S. have grown so accustomed to our opulence as a substitute for authentic joy. We think if we can just get a better lap top, DVD player, I-pod, Play station, Lexus, or new sofa for the living room, then our salvation would be complete, and our souls would sing. And that is never true.

In 1999 I spent two weeks in Colombia, with a delegation from the United Church of Christ. Colombia is an amazingly ravaged country. It suffers under the longest and bloodiest civil war in this hemisphere. It is torn by right wing paramilitaries, left wing guerrillas, and a corrupt, brutal government. Back in the early nineties both the right and left started taxing the cocaine drug trade, making millions and fueling the war. They say that today the rebel groups in Colombia are the best paid revolutionaries in the world.

Part of our stay was in a squatters' community outside of Florencia in one of the most war-torn, economically damaged parts of the country. My hostess was Maria Dorges, a lovely, dedicated church person, who had been widowed by the war and was a seamstress by trade. She had lived for many years in a smaller town out in the country, but because of the intensity of the fighting she and her children fled to this wretched "house" near the city that consisted of two small rooms with paper thin walls and no floor. She was charming and gracious, but had little to offer guests. There was no phone or running water, electricity only two hours a day, and the "bathroom" was an open commode up the hill behind a curtain. Nonetheless, she had a sweet air of grace and joy about her and she was a wonderful mother to two young sons who fought over which one would get to sit in our laps during our visit. There was a sense of hope and love in the family that overwhelmed and overturned their awful living conditions.

On Sunday she took us to her church, a vibrant, exhilarating community that celebrated their blessings in Christ in the midst of desolate economic conditions. The songs gave them power and the sermon gave them insight that I seldom experience in the U.S., even in my own church. They held hands and sang and prayed and then had an offering of letters to the mayor of Florencia to demand clean sewerage for their community. My delegation came from a country that worships mammon and controls its enemies. We're not used to a God who liberates the oppressed and says to love our enemies. At the end of the service we all left feeling filled with the Spirit, but while Maria was also energized and empowered, our delegation members were slightly depressed. Our church life at home was so impoverished next to hers. Her strength in God was so rich next to ours.

When night came, Maria offered us the twin beds of her sons and said they would sleep with her on the couch in the living room. I told her no, we would sleep on the floor; we couldn't take their beds. But she insisted. "You must sleep on a bed," she said. "You are our guests, you are used to beds, and also," her eyes twinkled, "our house has a small problem with snakes." We took the beds.

I had a terrible night. Her son's bed was a five-slat bed with two slats missing. It was surrounded with a mosquito net that sometimes worked and sometimes didn't. And sure enough all through the night I could hear a whispery, slithery noise of something gliding across the floor. I slept fitfully, falling through the slats and swatting mosquitoes. One time when I really had to go up the hill, I pulled on my boots and moved as rapidly and carefully as I could.

The next morning I awoke to the sound of Maria boiling coffee on her one-burner gas stove, with water she had gotten from a large tank outside the door, which is filled from a water truck once a month. The kids ran in laughing and screaming to greet their gringo guests. "How did you sleep?" she asked.

I looked around her room and saw pictures on the wall of family members in suits recalling a more pleasant age, coffee being served in small glasses because there was only one cup in the house, a chicken that walked across the floor fleeing from the neighbors who wanted it for dinner. I saw her beaming smile and magnanimous attempts at hospitality and generosity. "How did you sleep?" she asked again. I remembered that I would soon be boarding a plane to return to surround-sound music, central heat and air, box spring beds, and…fewer snakes. "How did I sleep?" I repeated back to her. "Yes," she said. "How was your bed?" I picked up one of her giggling young boys and hugged him and put him in my lap. "I slept fine," I said. "I slept just fine."